JEWISH REFUGEES IN SWITZERLAND DURING THE HOLOCAUST

Jewish Refugees in Switzerland during the Holocaust

A Memoir of Childhood and History

FRIEDA JOHLES FORMAN

VALLENTINE MITCHELL
LONDON • CHICAGO, IL

First published in 2009 by Vallentine Mitchell

Catalyst House,
720 Centennial Court, Centennial Park,
Elstree, WD6 3SY, UK

814 N. Franklin Street
Chicago, Illinois,
60610, USA

www.vmbooks.com

British Library Cataloguing in Publication Data

ISBN 978 0 85303 961 7 (cloth)
ISBN 978 0 85303 951 8 (paper)

Library of Congress Cataloging in Publication Data

To the memory of my parents, Malka and Kasiel Johles,

and my brother Max Johles, z'*l*,

to the future of my children Gideon and Jessica

and to my grandchildren, Yaneev, Annika, Mika and Dahn

CONTENTS

PLATES

*These pictures have been used to illustrate the cover of this book.

PREFACE

Papers, documents and photographs – the staples of refugee life – were scattered on a table in front of me at the archives of the Joint Distribution Committee in New York. I had come here, in 1999, to one of the major Jewish rescue organizations, hoping to find clues, traces of my life and the lives of thousands of others who had spent the war years in Switzerland. It was late in the afternoon, and I had already examined more than a hundred letters, memos and telegrams sent between Europe and the New York headquarters of the 'Joint', as it is known. From a 1943 folder, I pulled out a memo covered with pencil-marks and crossed-out lines; the heading, in bold print, read: 'These Escaped'. It continued: 'The JDC releases names of 100 Austrian Jews who fled to Switzerland.' My years of researching social movements had taught me that every document, even the seemingly insignificant, carries the potential for revelation. I scrutinized the list, but recognized none of the names that filled the first page; I hadn't expected that I would, now, more than fifty years after the event. Then, on the second page, I saw 'Johles', my family name: 'Johles, Kasiel, Johles, Malka, children, Max and Frieda'.

For that first instant, I could not breathe. I stared at the faint print, the worn grey paper. I was afraid to move, afraid these names, my names, would disappear. I knew no one at the archives to whom I could disclose this discovery. I had to wait for evening, when I was with my daughter; to her I could express the wonder of it: that of the thousands who had crossed into Switzerland to escape the Nazis, our names should have been noted in a memo that had travelled from one country to another, travelled across time, until it landed in the Joint office in New York. Adding to my amazement was the absence of my cousin and her family's names; we had crossed the border that night, clinging to each other. Why were our names on that list and not theirs?

For several years I had been considering writing about the Jewish refugees in Switzerland; I'd even begun the initial research, but the project had been put aside due to time constraints. Although I rarely succumb to providential messages, this was an omen I could not easily cast off or ignore.

The Swiss years, 1942 to 1946, loom larger than any subsequent years in my life. This was wartime and I was of an age, 5 to 9, when memory is alive and can be recalled later, not as a chronicle but as a patchwork of reminiscences. The unforgettable nature of that period was intensified by a sense of incongruity: that my family, who moved through the world with angst, whose every step at that time was taken with predictions of doom, should be among the Swiss, in their country of peace and tranquillity, with their utilitarian, efficient character. We were refugees in the fullest sense, the ultimate strangers, in contrast to the illustrious non-Jewish political refugees and intellectuals who could return to their countries after the war. Because we had come from Austria, and before that from Poland, repatriation was neither desirable nor possible. We were there because we were Jews and because we were the fortunate who had escaped.

The story of the Jewish refugees in Switzerland during the Second World War has been all but absent from Holocaust history, although close to 25,000 women, men and children spent the war, or some part of it, in that small, neutral country. Some historical and biographical works are available in French and German; these essential works, however, barely touch upon the details of the camps: their social organization, daily life, and cultural and religious activities. The documentation in English is so sparse that this aspect of the Holocaust is in danger of vanishing. Most of what we do have in English is made up of composite pictures: the mother and child; the man assigned to a labour camp; the elderly; the infirm. What is missing is the specificity of flesh and blood people, with pre-war lives and with unique responses to their fate.

Apart from the intrinsic value of this particular aspect of Holocaust history, we find in this Jewish refugee narrative a rare account of Jews in Europe who were not threatened with extinction. Once admitted to Switzerland, they could live as Jews. Amidst a Jewish world that was fast disappearing, these refugees were often able to conceive and plan a spiritual and intellectual future.

Hurled together by the war, the internees frequently had only the most tenuous of bonds; class and educational disparities, political and religious dissonance marked the community. And yet they had to coexist for an unspecified period and make a life for themselves and their children under severe, unfamiliar conditions.

The yearly Shoah memorials that I attended in Toronto always included a talk by a survivor of concentration camps or of living in hiding, but never the story of refugees in Switzerland. One year, at such a gathering, I decided that our experience had to come to light. Someone had to break the silence and if not now, when? My initial historical research confirmed my suspicion that this story had not yet received its due, certainly not for anglophone readers. I expected that in Toronto, with a sizeable population of Holocaust survivors, there would be former refugees who had spent the war, as I had, in Switzerland. I contacted a writer for the widely read *Canadian Jewish News*, who agreed to do an article on the subject, which would include a request to former refugees to call me. By then, I had a book in mind. The contribution of these interviews has guided my hand throughout, although few have been explicitly quoted in the text.

On the very morning of the weekly's publication, my telephone began to ring. A gravelly, smoker's voice, the trace of a German accent: 'I just read the article in the *Canadian Jewish News*. I was a refugee, too, in Switzerland.' The phone calls continued that afternoon and evening, in rhythmic succession. Some callers spoke of their own experience, while others told of parents, now dead, who had been in the camps but had disclosed only the vaguest details to their children.

I was unprepared for my past to return in such a sweeping way. After the briefest introduction we talked about the camps: which ones, when, with whom. By the end of the day, I was no longer myself; something had been released which I could no longer control. The project now had a life of its own, with its own cast waiting to speak their lines.

I needed time – for what I didn't know, but I had to escape or my heart would burst. I roamed from room to room like a sleepwalker. With these voices on the phone, their age and birthplaces immediately familiar, a segment of my life, my early childhood, was reappearing. We had a history that we shared with few survivors of the Holocaust. We, sojourners in Switzerland, were a tiny minority, now scattered across the world, with no formal links, no organizations like those for concentration camp survivors or displaced children.

It had been my hope that the article relating my war experience and current research on that subject would rally refugees, but now that they were here, I didn't know what to do. In a moment of clarity, I arranged to contact them again later on. But extracting ourselves from these conversations was not easy: we couldn't break away from each other; another name, another story had to be told right then, in outline at least.

My return calls to these people, simply to schedule time for an interview, proved to be more complicated than expected. In the course of giving me directions to drive to their homes, it became apparent to them that I would be using public transportation. An alarm was set off. 'You can't get to my house without a car', was a common response. I maintained that I always travelled by subway and bus and I would find my way this time too, but I was no match for them. 'I'll pick you up at the bus stop,' our conversation would conclude. Such solicitude and protectiveness came from people who, as children, had crossed borders, on foot, at night with the sounds of police dogs barking in the background.

A psychologist friend, expert in the art of interview, insisted that I prepare a questionnaire that would cover all aspects of these former refugees' lives: family memories before the Holocaust; the escape route to Switzerland; daily life in the camps; education; cultural and religious organizations; also such details as sleeping and eating arrangements. She instructed me in how to be patient and silent, how to resume after a tearful memory had been recounted, and how to keep the interview on track. My pages of notes contained messages in bold: 'Silence is okay, check tape recorder, take your time to complete all categories.'

The anticipation of my first interview threw me into a spin. Preparing for the trip to the suburbs took on such proportions that if I had been asked for my passport, I would not have thought it strange. I was crossing borders again, this time more temporal than spatial. As I checked and rechecked the tape recorder, packed extra batteries and tapes, notebook, photographs, and slippers in case of snow, a vaguely familiar sensation arose – I was a refugee once again. All the marks of one about to take flight were present: fear of the unknown, of saying the wrong word, of forgetting something important, as well as self-hypnotic messages of strength and courage. So began my contacts with those who had shared my life during the war years.

Judaism's exhortation to remember, never to forget, articulated first in biblical literature and continued through millennia to our day, was the unspoken tenet, which guided our discussions. We had chosen to remember and recount every word, every image. We could not leave out anyone or anything; we knew that leaving them behind meant we might never see them again, an all too familiar memory.

I have been referring to these meetings as interviews, but really they were encounters. I did not approach them as a social scientist; moreover, 'my people', as I began calling them, resisted the formats of objectivity and compliance. They had their own construction of events to which they constantly returned, even as I tried to keep the pre-established order. Charmingly undisciplined, they reminded me of the mischievous children we were in the refugee camp. My well-organized questionnaire was ignored and eventually disappeared. I remembered not to finish their sentences for them, not to interrupt, but these traces of professionalism aside, I was no longer in charge. They wanted to talk, to shape the discourse, to express the stories and events that compelled them: they responded sparingly to my issues and lavishly to their own posed questions.

I decided to bring my photographs of the camp in Morgins to every meeting, in part because I wanted to affirm a connection to my people. The photographs also served as identity papers of sorts. I was not there to record their wartime experience; it was a collaborative effort that I sought.

I knew beforehand that photographs would be brought out at a certain point in our meeting – at the end perhaps, as they are in well-orchestrated testimonies. Once again, however, the predictable pattern did not hold here; there was no tidy containment of images in albums or on mantelpieces. Paintings, photos, children's drawings and poetry all spilled over from one room to the next. Some were set in elegant frames, others merely affixed magnetically to the refrigerator, but the effect was the same. Enveloped by these images, I felt that I was inside an installation, time and space compressed.

Their histories were exhibited in the formal portraits of ancestors, sitting or standing erect: solemn figures. These photographs belonged to the lucky ones who had somehow salvaged their family mementos. The next generation, ours, appeared in black and white snapshots. That time frame included group shots of camp-mates from Switzerland, which evoked vivid, lovingly told stories and reminiscences, every name recalled. Children and grandchildren, in glossy colour prints, many enlarged, were exuberant, bold and at home in the world.

On the bus ride home, stiff from the strain of listening and nodding, I tried to find the common thread to all their stories and pictures. Slowly it came to me: no more hiding. They had surrounded themselves with their lives, their past and present. Where once they were confined, at times forced to conceal their identity, some of them given a new name or another religion, they were now free to live in the open: to be extravagant, even, in the display of their humanity.

Translation, from one language to another, from one period and culture to another, has always been part of my life. At the age of 5, I began to act as the interpreter for my parents, from French and, later, from English into Yiddish. As the necessity of transition became more frequent, their facility to move from one language to another lagged behind. It was a duty I found onerous but saw no way of avoiding.

Now, as I toil to transfer memory into narrative, I am once again in that strange, shadowy land of translation, balancing those two languages, the past and present – assuming the posture of a water-carrier with two pails. Somehow words must be fastened onto memories to bring them out of their inchoate existence. Traces of visual, sensual and oral recollections prepare for their next journey: to be seen, judged and perhaps understood.

ACKNOWLEDGEMENTS

During the years of research, interviewing and writing, I longed for the moment when my appreciation would be expressed; now the pleasure is mine to thank and acknowledge those who helped, encouraged, and critiqued:

Esther Sokolov Fine and Sharon Kirsh, my writing sisters, whose weekly presence illuminated my return to the past; for their heartening words and meticulous reading, their thoughtful advice and humour I will be forever grateful. Gail Geltner, for the delight of her company and her acute editorial sense. Claire Pizer, whose wisdom and tenacity helped me reclaim childhood experience. Erica Simmons, who provided advice and direction, always with wit and generosity. Paula Doress-Worters, my cousin who helped recapture the early years after Switzerland, continues her acts of dear friendship. Fritzi Rosner Shay, my cousin who crossed borders with me and facilitated my return to Switzerland on a research mission. Michèle Stroun, the kindred spirit with whom I reunited after 60 years. Bashert. Ruth Fivaz-Silbermann, whose serendipitous intervention transformed memory into reality. Nancy Lefenfeld, who shared her research and sparked a chain reaction. Marika Arban, Leah Bacon, Esther Israelski, Patricia Mills, Ann Pappert, Rusty Shteir, Richard Teleky, and Rachel Vigier who kept watch over my work with the eyes of wise critics and the abiding interest of friends. Aviva Cantor, for close reading and creative response. Erika Gideon Wyler, whose graciousness and generous hospitality opened remarkable possibilities during my research voyage in Zurich. Evie Mandel, who warmly shared her living quarters and gave pivotal advice during my stay in Geneva.

For their kind and expansive responses to my many questions about events long past in Switzerland, I thank: Germaine Goldberg, Marthe Gosteli, Stefan Herzka, Liselotte Hilb, Gabor Hirsch, Regula Ludi, Stefan Maechler, Jean Plancon and Samuel Jean Richard. To the wonderfully helpful staff at the Archiv für Zeitgeschichte, Zürich, ETH (Eidgenössisch Technische Hochschule) who made each day I spent there a time of wonder and reclamation; my thanks also to those geniuses who collected documents and the archivists who made them available. Claudia Hoerschelmann guided me through the vast archival holdings of modern Jewish history; she arranged meetings with former refugee workers, camp administrators, and others who could supply missing links, witnesses to those events. Sheldon Kirshner, whose timely article about my research catalyzed the response of former refugees. Former refugees open-heartedly allowed me to enter those difficult years with deep understanding of the importance of remembering and inscribing our shared experience as refugees in Switzerland: Varda Bernstein, Heini Bornstein, Ann-Helen Eidlitz, Renata Eisen, Serge Entine, Louise Fluk, Fee and Eric Goldfarb (turned back at the Swiss border), Liane Renee Klugerman, Brakha Scheinman, Adolph Schmidt, Vera Schweber, Michel Socha, Inge Spitz and Alice Stern Schmidt. Individuals who contributed in unique ways: Rafael Yossifov, Eileen Simmons, Lynn McClory.

I am very grateful for the research funding I received from The Memorial Foundation for Jewish Culture, Hadassah International Research Institute on Jewish Women, and Women Remember Association. Thank you to Heather Marchant, Joanna Lawson and Jenni Tinson at Vallentine Mitchell for their expertise and kind assistance at various stages of this project.

Author's Notes: The following are pseudonyms I have used to protect the privacy of certain individuals: Rabbi Klein, Madame Locafio, Madame Greenbaum and Hannah. All translations are the author's

1

INTRODUCTION

Why Switzerland? Why did Europe's Jews, endangered and hunted, seek refuge in this small country, surrounded as it was by Germany and Nazi-occupied lands? A confluence of factors contributed to its signature designation as a haven: its reputed neutrality and humanitarianism, its location and geography.

The history of Switzerland during the Second World War is complex and contradictory, and remains disputed. Since the nineteenth century, it has represented itself as a country where wartime neutrality was linked to a tradition of humanitarian asylum. Switzerland's cultural clichés, its childish delights – chocolates, yodels, cow bells, Heidi stories – and its images of innocence and tranquillity, of peace and bucolic bliss, contrasted sharply with the stark reality. Recent revelations by younger scholars, critical of the self-serving, government-approved portrayal of history, point to another picture, in which the commanding institutions of Switzerland were neither neutral nor humane.

During the war, Switzerland served as the financial centre of much of the world, owing to well-established banking practices with their structures of secrecy and confidentiality. While capital flowed freely, the stream of human beings was restricted. The gold of misery that the Nazis had extracted from murdered Jews and looted countries, sent for safekeeping to Swiss vaults, contributed to the German war machine. Converted swastika-marked gold bars were exchanged for universally accepted Swiss currency and credit. These financial dealings turned a handsome profit for the accommodating banks; at the end of the war, Switzerland emerged richer and more prosperous than any other country in Europe.

The Swiss Army, a powerful and revered institution, linked in mythic proportions to its independence, was heavily implicated in the government's indifference to the fate of Europe's Jews. The commander-in-chief of the Swiss Army, Henri Guisan, was an iconic figure, friendly to high-ranking Nazis. He eased the way for cooperation, whereby vitally needed parts for weapons were supplied, as were other materials (Guisan's son headed a factory that built the barracks sent to Germany for their concentration camps). Two-thirds of Swiss troops were demobilized to work in munitions factories, to increase industrial production for Germany's wartime economy. Estimates are that this collaboration extended the war by at least a year, contributing to the death of millions.

The Swiss press, for the most part liberal and anti-fascist, was heavily censored by a government ever-watchful lest information about its collaboration should leak to the Allies. Britain and the United States were suspicious of Swiss neutrality and threatened reprisal. Thus, although consular offices, government, banks and industry all knew details of the war and the Holocaust, the Swiss public, by and large, was kept in ignorance.

Under most circumstances neutrality is a deceptive position, taking cover under a cloak of equivalence. In the eyes of Switzerland, the parties at war, such as Nazi Germany and Great Britain, were seen as comparable. Were we to accept uncritically, to concede Switzerland's self-proclaimed epithet, to deny the mounting evidence of its collaboration with Nazi Germany, we would still be left with a major question: is neutrality in a context of genocide a morally acceptable position?

The Jews of Europe were not at war with any country; in fact, most of Europe waged war against the Jews. They were the victims of genocide, a deliberate and explicitly articulated Nazi policy. They were unprotected as civilians and citizens of Axis and occupied countries or, worse, zealously denounced to their pursuers. Yet, claiming neutrality, Switzerland refused safe haven to thousands, thereby contributing to crimes against humanity.

Switzerland's perception of itself as a benevolent country should certainly have been expressed in favour of the Jews during the Holocaust, but anti-Semitism played a decisive and pernicious role in Swiss refugee policy. Heinrich Rothmund, director of the Eidgenössisches Justiz- und Polizeidepartement (EJPD), the Police Division in the Federal Justice and Police Department, one of the architects of Swiss refugee policy, proclaimed: 'In order to prevent the rise of anti-Semitism, it is our duty to keep Jews out.'

Fearing a flood of Jewish refugees leaving Germany (which included Austria following the *Anschluss*, the annexation, in 1938), the Swiss instigated the introduction of the 'J' stamp on the passports of Jews to identify them as non-Aryans, thus acceding to the racial laws of the Nazis. The 'J' stamp was the Swiss equivalent of the yellow star that Jews were forced to wear in occupied Europe; it marked them as easy targets, sealing their fate and also endangering their escape to other countries.

The Swiss government knew about the 'Final Solution' early on in the war through its ubiquitous diplomatic and consular channels throughout Europe; the Geneva-based League of Nations and the International Red Cross further added to its position as a hub of information. Despite Switzerland's position as a nerve centre, xenophobia prevailed, and entry for Jews was severely curtailed during the most catastrophic period. 'The lifeboat is full' was a catchphrase for its refugee policy and implementation; its watchwords were *Verfremdung* (fear of foreign influence) and *Verjudung* ('Judaization'). Those persons who sought refuge 'solely on racial grounds' were explicitly denied the status of political refugees – that is, victims of political persecution. Nazi racial laws were not accepted as grounds for admittance. The reversal of Swiss refugee policy did not come until the Allies were close to victory, in 1944; it was then too late for most of Europe's Jews.

For those in flight, Switzerland's mountains and forests offered seamless borders with France, Italy, Austria and Germany, which were accessible on foot. At the same time, this geographic position created the popular fiction that the encircling Axis powers could easily invade Switzerland, putting it in jeopardy. There is scant evidence that accepting Jewish refugees would have impeded Swiss-German relations, which were forged through personal connections and ideological links between the Swiss ruling class and their Nazi counterparts.

The small, powerless Swiss Jewish community, numbering about 18,000, could do little to stem its country's historical anti-Semitism. For brief periods, following protests by church groups, socialists, liberal political parties, the media, and welfare organizations, restrictions at the borders were eased: 'hardship cases' – families with children under 16, pregnant women, the elderly and infirm – were allowed to enter. 'Instant families' – the attempts to share children with childless couples – did not always succeed in entering, and those who were detected were sent back. Although figures on Jewish refugees who were allowed entry are less than exact, their numbers never exceeded 30,000; most accounts hover at around 24,000 Jews.

For every Jewish refugee who crossed into Switzerland, at least as many, and by all estimates many more, were turned back or handed over to the Germans, to almost certain death. Having been denied visas by the Swiss consular offices in Nazi Europe, or having heard of the restrictions and closed borders, many did not even attempt the illegal crossing. Figures are often misleading; not all rejections were recorded during the war, and following the war, morally incriminating records were destroyed. Surviving documentation, however, indicates that

24,500 Jews were victims of *refoulement* – that is, they were turned back at the borders. Of the 300,000 foreigners (civilians, deserters, prisoners of war and fugitives) who spent the war years in Switzerland, at most 10 per cent were Jews. May we not call this a Jewish quota? In the calculation of human tragedy, the International Red Cross was not guilt-free. During the early years of the war, this highly respected agency denied Jewish children from other European countries a summer vacation in Switzerland, its well-established practice to benefit needy youngsters. The Red Cross showed neither remorse nor self-reproach in its explanation; it maintained that if these children were prevented from returning to their own countries, which were now at war, they would become refugees in Switzerland. The risk would simply be too great.

Tragically, the rescue of Jewish children was not a high priority even among the Allies. Britain stands out as having received 10,000 children from Germany and Austria in the *Kindertransport* but many were left behind, sharing the fate of the one-and-a-half million who were murdered by the Nazis and their collaborators. The United States admitted about 200,000 Jewish refugees from 1933 to 1945, most of them before 1941; compassion was not the prevailing spirit. Canada's villainous response to the plight of Europe's Jewish children is unmatched by any of the Allied or neutral countries. In the early years of the war and later, opportunities existed to spirit children marked for deportation out of France, if only a country would admit them. Canada was willing, indeed eager, to accept children from Britain, France, and Holland, provided they were not Jews. The lives of thousands of Jewish children could have been saved had Canadian immigration policy and its civil service been moved by conscience and pity, rather than by extreme expressions of anti-Semitism.

While the officialdom of Switzerland will not be inscribed in history among the righteous of the nations, many of its citizens did carry the mantle of humanity. Grateful as we are to those righteous Swiss citizens who did not turn their backs on Jewish refugees, we must also remember that they did not risk their lives as did the valorous who hid or protected their Jewish friends and neighbours in occupied countries. In Switzerland, punishment and condemnation, but not execution, were meted out to some individuals who used their position to help Jews. Paul Grueninger (1892–1972), honoured as 'Righteous Among the Nations' by Yad Vashem, rescued between 2,000 and 3,000 refugees. In his position as captain and commander of the St Galen cantonal police, he arranged for the illegal entry of Jews from Austria in

1938. That same year, he recommended an open refugee policy. For his humane intervention, he was dismissed from his post, criminally charged with dereliction of duty and tampering with official documents. A life of hardship and insecurity followed. Political and legal rehabilitation came only in the 1990s.

Another 'Righteous Among the Nations', Carl Lutz (1895–1975), Swiss Vice-Consul, head of the department representing foreign interests in Budapest, saved thousands of Jews by issuing group certificates for migration to Palestine. Lutz also issued letters of protection guaranteeing safety to those awaiting passage to Palestine. By 1944, close to 50,000 Jews lived under Swiss protection. Lutz also housed Zionist youth groups, enabling them to aid refugees and escapees from labour camps. In Budapest he is known as the Swiss Wallenberg. As late as 1949 his superiors in the federal government reprimanded Lutz for his actions; belated recognition for his life-saving intervention came in 1958.

Pastor Paul Vogt (1900–84), co-founder of Swiss Refugee Relief, used his considerable influence to defend the rights of refugees and to speak out against the heartless border restrictions. He was a vocal critic of Swiss refugee policy of separating families in internment camps. In 1952 he co-founded the Swiss children's home in Kiryat Ye'arim in Israel with Nettie Sutro (1890–1967), the tireless, dedicated director of the Swiss Relief Organization for Refugee Children.

Gertrud Kurz-Hohl (1890–1972), co-founder of the Swiss Refugee Relief, led the appeal in 1942, to ease entry restrictions for refugees. Clara Nef, president of the Federation of Swiss Women's Clubs, intervened on behalf of the Jews of Hungary in 1944, the year of mass deportations to Auschwitz.

Once admitted to Switzerland, Jewish refugees were quarantined in reception camps, where they were kept for weeks, sometimes months, depending on individual circumstances. In a specious act to insure efficiency, the Central Refugee Camp Commission ordered the separation of families. Men were consigned to work camps, replacing the Swiss workforce that had been drafted for home defence; they were forced into hard labour, clearing forests and building roads as well as doing agricultural work. Women were sent to family camps where they were assigned to the domestic sphere, providing laundry services, sewing and mending for the army, in addition to communal housekeeping.

Children under 16 years of age were sent to foster families, many of them Christian, or to children's colonies; the more fortunate were allowed to stay with their mothers in family camps. Older adolescents, young Zionists, were placed in *hakhsharot*, preparatory agricultural programmes for migration to Palestine after the war. Some boys were given the chance to further their studies at technical schools or universities. Girls were denied that privilege; domestic science and early childhood education were as close as they came to career development. In some cases, domestic science was a prerequisite for admission to teacher training courses.

Treatment in the camps chiefly depended on the camp administrators, many of whom were military personnel accustomed to army discipline, which they enforced without regard to the plight of the internees in their care. Limited freedom of movement, early morning *appels* (roll-calls) and punishment for minor infractions were common.

Many internees, from a wide range of humanity, contributed to the cultural life of the camps; actors, artists and musicians provided entertainment of a high professional calibre. Theatre productions spanned European classics: Goethe, Schiller (*Nathan the Wise* was a favourite) as well as familiar Yiddish plays. Virtuoso musicians and amateur choirs performed in the camps and were also invited to play for city audiences. Jewish cultural life was expressed in theatre and in series of lectures in the camps. Yiddish newspapers, published by the refugees, included camp news and reports from the rest of Europe, as well as literary reviews.

The Orthodox camps were rich in religious leaders and scholars eager to preserve Jewish life and provide spiritual comfort and guidance as well as education. The Sabbath and Jewish holy days were celebrated in traditional ways. Dietary laws (*kashrut*) were observed without great effort since meat was a rarity, and Passover food was provided by Jewish welfare organizations. Education continued to be integral to Jewish life: children's schooling included Hebrew, prayer, history and art, often taught by experienced teachers. Adults could attend Talmud and Bible classes in the evening.

For years Switzerland had been central to political Zionism (the movement to establish a Jewish homeland in Palestine), initiated by the first Zionist Congress held in 1897 in Basel. During the Second World War, a strong Zionist presence was felt in the camps and among Swiss Jews in the cities. Courses in Hebrew, the language of Zionism, were ubiquitous. Songs and dances expressing the longing and visions of pioneering work in Palestine were introduced at social gatherings.

Refugee relief during the war was a major preoccupation for the Swiss Jewish community. Faced with thousands of Jews who needed immediate and long-term assistance, welfare organizations, some already providing aid to the indigent, moved with alacrity and devotion. Volunteer work was the women's domain and they took upon themselves welfare work of all sorts; professionals and volunteers were the sustainers in refugee aid. Indeed, the picture that emerged was one of housekeeping and nurturing on a large scale, a female world with its mix of practicality, compassion and imagination.

The women who were central to the *Hilfswerk* (aid to refugees) had no vote federally and no broad political voice. They had to influence and implement programmes without the requisite authority. Many suffragists were involved in refugee work and their struggle for rights, at times, had to recede in favour of relief work. Associations of women teachers were among the first to participate in aid to children.

Swiss women, disenfranchised until 1971, played a primary role in the life and well-being of refugees, advocating the acceptance of Jews to Switzerland and heading a variety of welfare organizations that served the complex needs of a population which had been displaced, dispossessed and often traumatized. Their wards were most often children, some orphaned, and women, many of whom were alone. They carried on their work unstintingly with attention to countless significant details: proper placement for a child, care for a woman who was mentally or physically ill. Nor did they ignore the less urgent calls on their time such as Hanukkah gifts for every child and holy day needs such as Passover food.

The welfare volunteers, mostly homemakers, had scant authority or influence. When they wanted to hone their skills, to professionalize their work, they were discouraged by the Jewish organizations' establishment, whose male leaders claimed that Jewish women had no time for such luxuries. Despite the disparaging response to their request, the women succeeded, with the help of tenacious staff, in organizing workshops that taught proficiency in agenda keeping, report writing and efficient meeting procedures. Following workshops, an outpouring of letters to the organizers expressed gratitude and new-found confidence. Women were the lynchpins in welfare services, especially those to children. In administering refugee camps and children's homes, they stood out as moral beacons.

One administrator, Charlotte Weber, transformed a military internment camp into a collective community. She replaced the authoritarian, draconian structures with a democratic community where internees became residents who had a voice in the running of the camp. Charlotte Weber nurtured creativity through concerts, plays and the costumes sewn by seamstresses whose work had been limited to mending and darning for the men's camps. Even the kitchen staff were consulted on menus. With her refined sensibility, Charlotte Weber recognized that rehearsals for concerts were not equal to kitchen duty.

As the war drew to a close, the work of welfare agencies continued. Repatriation of refugees became a pressing matter for them and for the Swiss government. Vocational training programmes were organized across the country, in cities and internment camps. The Allied victory brought to the fore the need for Switzerland to restore its pre-war reputation as a benevolent society. More humane, sensitive measures toward the refugees were instituted; restrictions in camps were relaxed and refugee initiatives in camp management, so long denied, were encouraged. Greater autonomy and self-regulation were allowed in some camps. Psychological attention to the mentally ill and others in need of psychological help was now considered necessary, and to that end instructions were offered to camp heads.

For many refugees, Palestine was the only country that offered hope, but the doors remained locked by the British. Even after the Holocaust, countries continued to restrict the admittance of Jews: the US had a stringent quota system; Canada, already tainted by its war-time record towards Jews, did not open its borders in a generous welcome, preferring German farmers and Nazi war criminals; Poland was the site of 'peacetime pogroms' where thousands were murdered; Germany and Austria could not be considered sites for rebuilding shattered lives; and Switzerland was insistent on a Jewish exodus after the war.

Zionism was the most promising if not the only future for many young people. For the orphaned, the Movement became their family. Some young people came from families who had been Zionists before the war, in Eastern and Western Europe. Not all Jews in Switzerland were Zionists and those such as the Bundists, who were politically opposed to a Jewish homeland, did not remain silent in the passionate debates of the day. A compelling argument in favour of Zionism spoke to the immediate need of the many youngsters who were alone and homeless in the world: a community, providing them with a purposeful project, a new life as participants in settling the old-new land.

2

FROM LYON TO THE SWISS BORDER: 1942

1942

International Events
20 January: Wannsee conference to coordinate the 'Final Solution of the Jewish Question'.
27 March: First deportation of Jews from France to Auschwitz.
March to July: First transfers to extermination camps: Belzec, Sobibor, Treblinka, Auschwitz-Birkenau.
May/June: Introduction of the 'Jewish Star', the yellow armband in occupied Western Europe.
2 July: Deportation of non-French Jews from France.
16 July: Round-up and deportation of more than 11,000 Jews in Paris.
First deportations of Jews from Belgium to Auschwitz-Birkenau.
26 August: Large-scale round-up of Jews in unoccupied France.
11 November: The German Army occupies southern France.

Swiss Refugee Policy
July: Despite his knowledge of the extreme danger facing Jews, Robert Jezler, a member of the legal staff of the EJPD, drafts a report to the Swiss Federal Council on Refugee Development, which results in harsher practices of turning back refugees at the borders.
13 August: An EJPD bulletin mandates the expulsion of all civilian refugees at the border: 'refugees solely for reasons of race, for example Jews' are not considered political refugees.
25 August: An EJPD bulletin orders the temporary liberalization of the practice of expulsion.
30 August: Head of the EJPD, Councillor Eduard Von Steiger, first uses the metaphor of the 'overcrowded lifeboat'. He carries large responsibility for Swiss refugee policy.
22–23 September: Debate on refugee policy in the National Council.
October: The Police Division and church officials agree on the periodic creation of a *non-refoulement* list (of persons who are not to be expelled).

14 October: The International Committee of the Red Cross rejects the idea of a public appeal against violations of international humanitarian law.
21 October: Heinrich Rothmund, Director of the EJPD, which includes the Police for Foreigners, visits Sachsenhausen concentration camps during his three-week stay in Berlin. Rothmund is primarily responsible for Swiss refugee policies.
29 December: The EJPD makes acceptance of refugees more restrictive.
30 December: The International Committee of the Red Cross decides on measures for deported persons.

International Actions and Responses
August: The US State Department prevents the publication of information on the existence of extermination camps.
8 August: Gerhart Riegner, director of the Geneva office of the World Jewish Congress, informs the Allies about the 'Final Solution'.

(Information from Independent Commission of Experts Switzerland – Second World War, Jean-François Bergier, Chairman, *Switzerland and Refugees in the Nazi Era*.)

Borders, crossings, frontiers – words that today have multiple, metaphoric meanings – were literal life or death determinants in 1942, when I was 4 years old and living in Lyon, in the as-yet-unoccupied part of France. Years later, I came to realize the significance of that time and place when Klaus Barbie, 'the butcher of Lyon', commanded the fate of the Jews in that city. By 1942, my parents and I, along with my 15-year-old brother Max, had crossed the borders westward, the escape route of so many thousands of refugees fleeing the Nazi occupation: from Vienna, shortly after *Kristallnacht* in 1938, to Brussels via Aachen in Germany and, following the Nazi invasion of Belgium in 1940, to unoccupied France. We were on one of the last trains.

I recollect the details of our various flights from my father's accounts several years after the war. His stories were usually told on Friday nights when the cares of the workaday week were put aside and, according to Jewish tradition, were replaced by a spirit of sanctity. Sitting at the head of the table in the kitchen of our home in Boston, sated after the customary festive meal, my father leans back in his chair and loosens his belt. Gazing at the flickering Sabbath candles, he turns reflective, pensive. I am familiar with this fugue and I want him back with us at the table. I lure him into the present by plying him with questions about the past: 'How did we escape from Vienna? How did we get past the police?'

My father's eyes alight, as in one about to reveal the missing pieces of a mystery, he turns his face to me and begins to re-enact the incident at the border in Aachen.

'You were just a baby, one year old; it was a bitter winter night in December, the coldest in years; I held you close to me, inside my coat.' He crosses his arms in a cradling motion. 'At the checkpoint, we were stopped by a Gestapo who proceeded to interrogate us. As if on command, you began to wail. "What does she want?" ' My father mimics the Gestapo's hard, impatient tone. '"She wants her *lutchka*, her pacifier", I answered.'

Papa continues his story, adjusting his voice and posture to designate each speaker. '"Well, give it to her", he barked. I put the *lutchka* in your mouth, you stopped your crying and with a wave of his hand, the Gestapo dismissed us.'

My mother, who repudiated all reminders of the war, could not bear the review of our wanderings and close escapes; at the first sign of this ritual, she would leave the table. My brother, in Israel at that time, appeared in these stories only as a character, albeit a central one. That left Papa and me engrossed in a world we would not abandon.

My own earliest memories begin in Lyon, 1942, in a decaying, pauperized working-class district. For over five decades, I held on to that place, the name of which I remembered only as slurred, meaningless syllables, 'Kayserain,' which over time began to sound like the song, 'Que sera, sera'. Often I wondered whether I had fabricated the name. Then, a few summers ago, at a garden party in Toronto, I was introduced to a woman about my age, who came from Lyon. As we chatted, I related as vividly as I could certain episodes of my childhood during the war; I described our Lyon neighbourhood with a name that had clung all these years, Kayserain.

'Was there such a place with that name?' I asked. Anticipating a perplexed, furrowed brow, I was prepared to put an end, finally, to this mythical name.

'Oh! You mean, Quay de Serain, the area along the Serain River. Yes, it's still there and still as grimy and run down as ever.' Her quick and easy response emboldened me. Yes, there was such a place and, though slightly abbreviated, I had remembered its name.

That chance meeting in Toronto gave me ground to stand on; it meant my retrospection of those young years had substance. I could now trust myself to begin reconstructing the past. I have often pondered why accuracy is so vital. Why is giving a name so fundamental to creating order out of chaos? Where does the shift from memory to certainty occur: from the ephemeral, perhaps fabrication, figment, or fiction, to that moment of confirmation, when I can say: yes, that really did happen, I was there.

From infancy into my ninth year, I lived the life of a refugee, albeit a fortunate one amongst that group of humanity in flight. My parents and I were not parted for any extended period and although we did not fit into the usual domestic pattern, I felt myself the centre of their world. Our closeness made all the difference in my experience of those years. Yet family solidity, loving in every expression, could not bring me the security that comes from being at home – in a neighbourhood, on a street, in school with a best friend and favourite teacher – and from a continuity that can be taken for granted. Discontinuity itself was the continuous strand in my life as a refugee child. Like all children who come to consciousness deprived of that sense of at-homeness in the world, who experience only disruption, I remembered no 'then', no 'there', before our displacement. Adult refugees, on the other hand, carried with them temporal and spatial memories which could be recalled and revived, a potential balm during upheaval and dislocation. The imprint of their former lives also coloured and shaped their adult responses to their ordeal as refugees, and often represented a model for rebuilding an interrupted life, a future when the war would end.

A succession of cameo appearances, with colour and texture, come into view as I relocate myself to Lyon. We lived in dilapidated, squalid quarters, the exterior and interior of which complemented each other: up three flights of narrow, crooked stairs were our two cramped rooms, a kitchen and bedroom, forever grey and foggy, looking onto an outhouse in the courtyard. On the ground floor lived the communist family who hid us during the days of widespread round-ups of Jews. They were taking a risk by this good deed, especially since a child's cries would endanger everyone. I see myself in their dark room, lying in bed; Papa is smiling sympathetically at me. This must have been a short time before we crossed the border.

This miserable setting did not seep into my daily life, nor interfere with many normal childhood adventures. I attended the local *l'école maternelle*, a nursery school that I recollect with tenderness, and that belied the actuality of a world at war. At Christmas time, the nursery school distributed gifts to all the children, and I received a little stuffed dog; stitched of stiff, blue-grey military cloth, he carried himself with great dignity. I was too young to know that Christmas was not my holiday, and I was very pleased with my new companion. Not everyone was as lucky as I was to receive a toy; most of my playmates had to settle for hand-knitted socks, mittens and scarves. Hugging my treasure, I overheard two teachers whispering, 'What a pity to give children such practical gifts at Christmas time.' Did I receive a toy rather than mittens because the teachers, knowing I was a refugee, singled me out for such largesse? That gesture has stayed with me as a model of imaginative generosity and, to this day, toys have held a special, almost fetishistic, place in my life.

Providing my children with playthings when they were young was among my most gratifying acts of mothering, and this pleasure continues into the next generation. Anticipating delight, my steps quicken as I approach a toyshop; I am buoyant. From the moment I cross the threshold, my careworn persona recedes, my burdens slip away. It is not nostalgia that draws me to the time of my childhood, when playthings were an extravagance I could not even have considered to be within my reach. Now, in the guise of a doting maternal figure searching for the perfect gift, I survey the inhabitants of this enchanted land; I rush past the boys' artefacts and head toward the domestic realm of the girls, where dolls reign supreme. These inanimate objects intoxicate me: human size or miniature, porcelain or plastic, luxurious or plain, they speak to me. I hold and examine each doll, her accessories, the furnishings and accoutrements.

Even in wartime, I was an indulged child; 'No' was not a word my parents often used. Nonetheless, like most children of that time and place, I knew enough to make only modest material demands. My mother, especially, could not resist me. If I tired during our walks, she would carry me, a sturdy 4-year-old, for the rest of the way home. 'Why are you lugging such a big girl?' our French neighbours would gently reprove her. 'She wants me to', my mother would reply, unruffled. My own approach to child-rearing and other ways of being in the world come from her; in later years, my mother and I shared a disdain for the overly-disciplined.

There are incidents that today would be considered benign neglect on the part of my mother, but I cherish them as my adventures, as early indicators of a free spirit. One afternoon, refreshed from a nap, I slipped away, leaving my sleeping mother undisturbed. I walked myself to nursery school oblivious or unconcerned that I had no underpants under my short little dress. Soon my mother arrived with the necessary completion to my outfit and everyone treated that immodest episode with good humour.

I was unaware that life was not as it should be, and indeed for me it was still running as desired. One warm, sunny day, I was settled on a low stone wall at the quayside, a short distance from my mother and brother. Absorbed in conversation, my guardians did not notice that I had walked away with the scissors my mother had in her sewing satchel, which, in any case, she brought along mainly for the sake of appearance. With abandon I cut chunks of my hair, leaving no part untouched. Mama and Max laughed heartily when they saw my new hairdo and tried to correct the damage; placing a bowl on my head, they followed its outline and straightened what was left of my hair. Years later, I learned from a comic strip that the bowl method was the preferred way of cutting children's hair in America, a discovery which revived that hirsute moment in Lyon.

My light-hearted days came to an end early one morning in April 1942. Roused from sleep by a loud, persistent knocking on the door, my father turned to my mother lying next to him in bed, and whispered to her, 'They're here.' He hesitated, then opened the door to two plainclothes policemen. The raids, the round-ups of Jews in unoccupied France, had begun. Max seemed to know they'd come for my father. I didn't know why they were here, but I knew something bad was happening to us. Few words were exchanged: no screams, no entreaties, no wailing. We three stood silent as we watched my father. Papa was allowed to wash before being taken away. This act of dignity allows me to remember him in the dawning light, standing at the kitchen washbasin in his trousers and undershirt. My father, who prayed every morning, was not permitted that act of his morning rites.

Walking between his captors, Papa left in silence. As soon as the door closed behind them, Max dressed. 'I'll see if I can find out from the police station where they're taking Papa', he said, as if it were an everyday question. Then I was alone with my mother who had no soothing words for me, no assurance that Papa would be all right. I watched her put on her stockings, pulling them slowly over her feet and legs, stepping into her shoes. I dressed myself.

My mother held my hand as we walked from one house to another. She informed relatives and friends that my father had been picked up by the *gendarmerie*. 'Hide, while you still can, while there's still time', she urged and pleaded. Her warning calls were made without tears, without hesitation. In her brown oxfords her steps were purposeful and quick. Hardly speaking to me, she stared straight ahead, as though obeying some invisible force. We later learned that her action had saved several men from deportation.

In 1981, while sitting *Shiva*, in mourning for the loss of our father,

Max and I had time at last to relive the past. Max recounted the circumstances of our father's reappearance in Lyon four months after his deportation; his return to us had seemed like magic to me then, when I was 4 years old. Because of Max's fluent French and blond hair, he was able to pass as just another French boy; he cycled undetected to the work camp in Savigny, where our father was interned and, once there, succeeded against great odds in convincing the camp head to grant our father medical leave for a hernia operation. That operation probably saved his life, but not because of the medical intervention. During the weeks he was in the hospital, his camp had been liquidated, and most of the internees sent to the east.

I asked my brother how a 15-year-old Jewish boy was able to prevail at a time when pity for Jews was a rarity. Max responded: 'The commander was not a monster, they weren't all cut of the same cloth, you know. Perhaps I looked like one of his own sons. Also, I brought a beautiful, leather handbag for his wife.' Refusing to acknowledge his own courage, my brother's hands and face were posed in speculation: 'Who knows?' he concluded.

There is another thread to this fateful episode: while in the hospital, a priest who belonged to the Resistance approached my father with an offer to take him over the Pyrenees, to the safety of the Spanish border. Papa refused because he could not have taken his family on that arduous crossing.

Papa and I were the advance troops at the farm of the *passeur*, the guide, who would lead us to the Swiss border. My mother, brother and other family members were to join us the next day. We spent the night, my father and I, in the hayloft of the farmer's barn. I recall my father's solicitude and the intimacy of that night – an adventure we two were sharing, the first of many such moments in my childhood. He understands me, I thought to myself.

The next day was grey and damp, not at all propitious for a night crossing. We waited for the others to arrive, passing the time walking around the farm, holding hands, afraid to stray too far lest we arouse the suspicion of neighbours. Finally, late in the afternoon, the others arrived in an ambulance, a camouflage which my brother had somehow procured for the journey to the *passeur*'s farm, located a few miles from the Swiss border. Seven people climbed out of the ambulance; the air was charged. I saw my mother step down from the ambulance, a bewildered look on her face. This was the same expression I was to see often, on her and in photographs of people arriving at concentration camps in cattle trains. Was she anticipating the worst, the fate that could so easily have been hers? Safe for the moment, but for how long?

Moments after our group arrived, whilst they were still huddled outside, another car pulled up to the farmhouse. A pair of plain-clothes French police officers commanded us to move indoors. I ensconced myself in a corner of the capacious kitchen and observed the scene before me, where a heated discussion was taking place. Unaware that my life was in question, I sat as if at a theatre performance; one of the police, pointing to me and smiling, said '*Quelle mignonne*' (What a darling).

It was at my daughter's wedding in Israel that Max, who astonished everyone with his memory, furnished the details of what took place at that farmhouse in France, fifty-six years earlier.

'A man who came with our group, a former soldier in the French Army, pleaded with the police: "What will you gain by turning these people, these children, over to the Germans?" His words, or maybe our predicament, softened them.' Max continued with additional details: 'We gave them a gold watch, money, and after a few glasses of wine, they agreed to let us go. At the same time, they told the farmer that this was the last group of refugees he would conduct to the border.'

That night, on 26 September 1942, we began our trek from the French border into Switzerland. Our little assembly of nine consisted of my family of four, my 6-year-old cousin Fritzi and her parents, and an elderly couple who completed the appearance of a typical extended family. A downpour of rain, which continued through the early hours of the next morning, turned the forest floors and fields into muddy, slippery ground. Still recovering from his recent operation, my father could not carry me and I trudged on my own for much of the way. I overheard a whispered warning to one of the other men, not to take me on his back lest I fall asleep. We walked; people fell, got up, and continued. The elderly woman kept rolling over, stumbling under the weight of her many layers of clothing, stopping us all while she regained her footing.

Closer to the Swiss border, we heard the sounds of howling dogs. We stopped. We sat under a tree and waited for a quiet interval before resuming our march. In my recent interviews with former refugees who crossed the border on 26 September – a busy day on the Swiss frontier – a similar scene was described: night, rain, dogs. I recall that at some point, near the end of the crossing, we stopped at a house. Heavily laden looks were exchanged between the farmer and his wife, and soon the border police arrived. My cousin Fritzi related that moment in a publication on refugee testimonies: 'The friendly farmer's wife gave us milk, and newspapers to insert into our wet clothing. In the meantime the farmer notified the *Grenzpolizei* [the border police]. Quickly they arrived and interrogated us. The families that had children were allowed to stay. The childless couple was returned to France. This had been their second attempt to enter Switzerland.' (Newman, *Swiss Wartime Work Camps*)

My cousin and I continue to differ in our interpretations of events: she views the Swiss in a somewhat benign light while I recall more of the dark moments of those years.

On 26 September 1942, the day we crossed into Switzerland at the border village of Avussy, near Geneva, the EJPD passed new directives with the approval of the Federal Council. Applicable to the Geneva frontier, the categories were more refined than in earlier edicts but the principle remained the same. While individual border police may have chosen mercy when faced with refugees seeking asylum, most abided by the letter of the law:

I. Foreigners entering illegally must be turned back.
II. Those not to be turned back:
A: Deserters, if they can prove it, with at least a piece of uniform, a record of military pay or any other piece of identity.
B: Political refugees, that is, foreigners who from the outset, and of their own accord, expressly indicate such, and can offer a credible declaration.
Those who fled for reasons of their race are not political refugees conforming to the practice adopted on this day. [Italics mine]
C: In cases where turning back would cause a measure of extreme hardship:
1: Sick people, pregnant women
2: Refugees over the age of 65 (the spouses who have not reached that age are not to be turned back)
3: Unaccompanied children under 16 years of age
4: Parents with their own [underlined in original text] children under 16 [the category which applied to my family]
5: Refugees who from the outset, and of their own accord, make claim to have close relatives in Switzerland (spouse, father and mother, children), or in close connection with our country (a long-term stay).

> FRENCH JEWS [capital letters in original text] must be turned back without exception, given that they do not risk danger in their country.
>
> [The round-up of French Jews had already begun in March 1942.] (Fluckiger and Bagnoud, *Les Réfugiés civils et la frontière genevoise*.)

The directives to be enforced at the borders reflected the Federal Council's changing refugee policy in 1942. Fully aware of the extreme danger Jews were facing, a harsh expulsion practice was in place early in the summer. Later that summer, media censure brought about a temporary liberalization of expulsion practice. At the end of that year, the EJPD once again restricted acceptance of refugees.

Established in 1901, *Israelitisches Wochenblatt für die Schweiz/Journal Israelite Suisse* (the Swiss Jewish weekly) was a full-sized illustrated newspaper. It was the voice of the Jewish community, offering an intimate glimpse into Jewish life in Switzerland: organizational activities, cultural and religious life, social announcements and, during the war years, detailed accounts of refugee life.

The issue of 25 September 1942 (one day before we crossed the border) reflected the deep concern of the Jewish community in an article titled, 'The Refugees in Switzerland':

> At a board meeting of the Justice and Police Department, Federal Councillor Von Steiger urged cooperation between federal, cantonal and refugee organizations in finding a suitable balance between humanitarian imperatives and the understandable interests of the state. But as in his earlier official reports, the dogma of sustainability was again presented. The stream of refugees was 'painted black on black'.
>
> On the one hand, Councillor Von Steiger admitted to hesitation and difficulty; on the other he found it necessary to point out that not all immigrants were grateful and content, as though people for years dislocated and now hounded to death could be judged by the same standards as happy arrivals during normal times!
>
> More astonishing still, the fulmination that 'clandestine refugees' – such wonderful police-German – could be sent back to prevent the mounting increase in sustainable numbers. One may be curious about the reverberations of such talk, which can

> be said, without exaggeration, easily evaded public opinion. The hope remains still, that no measures will be taken against those who have already entered. According to Von Steiger's report, the number of 'covert' arrivals since April was close to 2,000, including 733 since September 1. It was often expressed in the press, especially in letters to the editor, that the number of refugees must not be an issue.

The 9 October 1942 issue of the Jewish weekly reported that two Jews in flight froze to death on the mountains. In another story from France, a mother and child threw themselves from the window rather than face deportation. An appeal for a humanitarian response pointed to Sweden as a model.

Israelitisches Wochenblatt, 16 October 1942: 'The campaign for refugee relief raised 12,000,000 SF. A week of refugee action: to raise money, moral awareness. The tradition of Swiss Asylum was invoked. Jewish organisations have carried the burden for years and cannot do it alone any longer; humanitarian solidarity is sought. Pastor Paul Vogt tells of the reception camps, where many arrive ill; help is urgently needed.'

These documents and newspapers which I found in the Swiss archives provided me with the background and context to my memories of 1942. They express the tragedies in Nazi occupied Europe and the urgent response of the Jewish community and its supporters in Switzerland.

3

GENEVA: 1942

In recounting the year I spent in Geneva as a refugee child, I fear I am about to commit a sacrilege: that in the midst of unspeakable horror and devastation I should be depicting days of beauty and mirth, innocent mischief, youthful discoveries – essentially, the very aspirations we have for all children. My days there were surely not all sunny and brimming with happiness, but they were within the realm of ordinary childhood with its mix of misery and joy.

It is not 'survivor's guilt' I experience when I allude to my good fortune in escaping to Switzerland and to Geneva in 1942. Rather, it is an inextricable bond I feel with those who were turned back at the border. By a stroke of misfortune, on that particular day when entry restrictions were more severe, when refugee policy was more brutal, they took the same path, the same direction that we did, but they were caught by the Swiss authorities and turned back to almost certain death. I can never forget how thin the line was between survival and death, and such knowledge inhibits a solipsistic account.

My love of cities, my deep attraction to them, had its genesis in Geneva, and to this day urban life remains identified with asylum, haven, sanctuary and refuge. The construction and the spacing of cities, and particularly the tension in the air: all these aspects have left an indelible mark on me. The larger the city, the more urban, the more urbane, the safer I feel. Geneva was radiant and seemed to radiate from a particular centre in which I placed myself; being there, I felt endowed with the sense that I was taking part in a grand enterprise. The city itself was a work of art, backed by the natural beauty of Lake Geneva and Mont Blanc. It was architecturally very much a European city in its layout, and in the age and solidity of the buildings; the design of parks and streets was a tribute to the love of public space.

Walking between my parents, holding their hands, I see our route again: through the old city, its dark, narrow, cobblestoned streets lined with tiny shops, their windows filled with sundries which were, at that time, so far out of my reach they seemed to emanate from a world altogether separate from the one I inhabited. The Swiss affection for miniatures gave me the dimension of a giant in the land of Lilliput. And then, at the end of an alley-like street, an opening came into view, the modern zone of the city with open, generously-scaled avenues and ubiquitous bridges.

That was 1942. By then, most of Europe was under Nazi occupation, and Jewish civilization on that continent was vanishing. Jews were being deported to their deaths from most European countries. Geneva, however, was visibly untouched, with no signs of devastation or adversity; it was a working city.

I was almost 5 years old in September, when we first arrived in Geneva as illegal refugees from France, just escaping the round-up of Jews and their deportation to the east. A few days after our arrival, we were assigned to temporary refugee quarters, a dark, dingy room in l'Hôtel du Soleil; its name notwithstanding, few rays of sun passed through the grimy windows while we were there. Grateful for asylum, we passed several months under the watchful eye of the local police, to whom we were required to report weekly, proving we had not escaped from our city of refuge.

Our next dwelling was a ground-floor apartment on the fashionable Rue de Lausanne, a broad street stretching from the central railroad station to a luxuriant park on the lake. To this day, although I am immersed in all the detailed, official documentation of our stay in Switzerland, I still cannot unravel the story of how we came to be so blessed. Compared to all our previous dwellings, our apartment was a place of splendour. We lived like human beings: a kitchen, indoor toilet, even parquet floors, which my father zealously polished to such a high gloss that my mother, unaccustomed to skating on ice, slipped and broke her arm.

The grand park at the end of our street was our second home; it offered my mother the respite she so badly needed and provided me with a constant source of merriment. In my informal observation of playgrounds across several continents, I have yet to find one as captivating as that one in Geneva. A particular amusement stands out in my memory: a maypole with metal chains and rings through which we put one leg and, with momentum generated by the riders, were propelled into the air; it was an act of cooperation, of collective movement.

'Rayzele', a Yiddish song I learned in Switzerland, I have remembered all my life because it is bound to a larger story. It is a musical dialogue between two lovers, Rayzele and Dovidl, as they carry on their courtship under the watchful eye of her mother. I loved this song. My

Tante Rosa – Rayzele was her Yiddish name – was my favourite aunt, my father's sister. I was always ready to perform for my parents, and even for a larger audience than these two beaming approval at every note. At the time, I surely didn't catch all the layers of meaning in that love song, but I knew it expressed love; it was in Tante Rosa's name and I wanted to court her. I sang it for her every time we came together and she too sent beams of love to me.

Tante Rosa had been only a hazy presence when we lived in Lyon; the night of the border crossing, she was a whisper in the background. It was in Geneva that our bond developed when she came to take care of me while my mother was in hospital for one of her frequent operations. I was 5 years old and we were living at 53 Rue de Lausanne in Geneva. Tante did all my bidding in a spirit of happy resignation; she was also my companion, if not my accomplice, in transgressive acts. After sunset one evening, we set out for the park near our apartment, a park that even in wartime overflowed with richly patterned flowerbeds, and was clearly marked off-limits. I simply asked her, no wheedling required, to pick a few flowers for me. I'd had my eyes on some perky tulips for days and I coveted them. Tante Rosa delicately climbed over the little fence, looked around sheepishly, and picked the tulips for me. We hurried home undetected, Swiss neutrality untouched. That act of defiance, that illegal moment in my young life, has stayed as a sweet taste for a lifetime.

During the weeks of Tante Rosa's stay, I entered into another conspiracy, one I would not have dared with anyone but her. I announced to the children in the park that my father owned a toyshop and that if they came to my house, they could have their pick. Later that day one little boy arrived with his older sister. I was exposed, but my aunt protected me and laughed it off as another bit of mischief created by her niece.

Those weeks with just the two of us, my aunt and I, set the tone for our relationship for years to come. Time and place changed but she remained for me a figure of constant acceptance and unstinting affection. Years later, in New York, she opened her apartment door to me, a 19-year-old from Boston and from an over-protective family, embracing me in the fullest sense. That act gained her little favour with my family, who believed that an unmarried daughter's place was at home, not in the wild city of New York.

'Rayzele' continued to appear in my adult life. At every Yiddish song circle, where it was a favourite, both melody and lyrics conjured up my childhood in Switzerland. Recently I came across my aunt's song in

Charlotte Weber's memoir, *Gegen den Strom der Finsternis* (Against the Charge of Darkness). Weber, a creative and compassionate camp administrator, recalls and reproduces that very song, which the women sang while at work. How I wished I could phone Tante Rosa to share this moment, but she had passed away a few years earlier.

Several years before my research journey to Switzerland, I had written about a family whose presence for close to sixty years had been a vivid and cherished memory, and a memory I thought it would remain. Reconciled to a life in which my past would never be brought back to me by the sight of a familiar face, I came to Geneva to search for documents of the Holocaust refugee community and, in the process, perhaps uncover traces of my own trail.

On Friday morning, 9 November 2001, at the appointed hour, I met with Ruth Fivaz Silberman, a historian working at the State Archives in Geneva, an ancient fortress-like structure encaved in the Old City, just a short walk from where my parents and I had lived before and after our internment in refugee camps. Over a simple but expensive lunch, we exchanged life stories. Born in Switzerland, the child of refugees, Ruth was now engaged in researching and documenting the incidents of *refoulement*, the turning back at the borders of thousands of Jews during the most disastrous years of the war.

By the second glass of wine, time and history compressed, a bond was established between us, and I recounted the events of my childhood to Ruth. Woven into my narrative with its many detours, I recalled a series of related incidents; some were personal recollections while others had been revealed just days earlier in my family files that had been meticulously stored for over five decades in the Archives for Contemporary History in Zurich. The files disclosed that a few months after our arrival in the refugee camp in Morgins, my mother, who was plagued by multiple health problems throughout her life, had to undergo a goitre operation. The correspondence in her file noted in great detail her objection to a clinic in the nearby village of Monthey. Mama insisted on a Geneva hospital for this procedure, perfected by the Swiss due to the frequent occurrence of the condition there. Indeed, for the rest of her life she had a delicate stitch across her throat; both cause and cure were her Swiss souvenirs. Back and forth the letters flew, from the camp to the central administration in Bern, until the authorities finally relented, provided that my mother would pay the difference.

The next hurdle involved me: Mama refused to leave me in the camp during her hospital stay despite everyone's urgings that such an arrangement would be best. At this time, my father was in the work camp in Sierre, where he had been interned since we had been forced to leave Geneva. My mother's will once again prevailed and she was permitted to take me with her to Geneva, but not before she earned the reputation of being a difficult, stubborn woman. 'She has a very unpleasant characteristic of pushing her objectives', recorded the camp administrator. Every history has its unsung hero; in my parents' life it was a welfare worker with the Jewish Immigrant Aid organization, by the name of Michèle Smidoff, who consistently intervened on their behalf with the compassion and imagination of an iconoclast. He wrote to the central administration: 'Mrs Johles is determined to take her child with her to Geneva. It is actually very understandable that she would want the child near her during her hospital stay.'

I continued telling my story to Ruth, describing in some detail the family who provided me with a home while my mother was hospitalized.

'I recall our first meeting with the Feuerwerker family in their apartment facing the central railway station in Geneva. Heavy, dark mahogany furniture and high ceilings gave it weight and substance, clutter, the signs of settlement. Something about it made me feel at home; there was a "there", as Gertrude Stein once described a city she loved. Their apartment evoked "thereness", where I could firmly place my feet, where I could stand; I knew I could stay there, be there, because the Feuerwerker family, who seemed to have been born to their home, matched its solidity. The parlour windows were large but I got no sense of sun streaming in; by now, I had accepted that dark places were to be my lot; this room had enough darkness for me to feel at home and yet not crush the spirit. It was solidity I grasped onto: that something would hold me, that I would be safe.

'After Mrs. Feuerwerker and my mother exchanged a few words, my mother turned to me and asked where I wanted to stay. I sensed desperation in her voice and tone. Was this her last option for me? Had she tried to place me in other homes and failed? I stood, staring out of the window facing the bustling, crowded street and said: "*du*" (here) in Yiddish. And so my mother left me with the Feuerwerker family. I don't remember the moment of her departure nor a farewell and I resist speculating about the cause of this amnesia.

'Why did I feel an immediate comfort with this family? Did they stand for the grandparents I never knew? I know I felt that I belonged. There was always a sense of imminent hysteria, a disposition that was familiar.

My own family's hysteria was quieter, theirs was more expressive, because they had less to fear, I suppose. I thought that this was the way people lived in the world, that this was the way they expressed themselves: that there was no tranquillity in people's comings and goings.

'Despite their stormy temperament, I felt a calm with them, although they were anything but a calm family. The patriarch, whose status and stature complemented each other, was tall, almost burly, with a grey-white beard, and always wore a skullcap, an open-collared white shirt and a black vest. He was in a constant state of rage, at the world and at those around him: his short, very round wife, his tall, slender, bird-like daughter. Authoritarian, Rabbi Feuerwerker ruled over the family, but by consent; no real terror was ever cast over the household. Mrs Feuerwerker wore a *sheitel* (peruke) and, as I recall, always an apron. She was no submissive presence but he set the dominant tone. I, however, was exempted from his outbursts. I followed him around the house, even into the bathroom when he performed his ablutions. I especially loved to watch him snipping his nasal hairs; I would stand on my toes and look up into his nostrils, gazing as deeply as I could at the small scissors as they clipped away.

'Occasionally I would be sent to spend the day with their grandchildren who lived close by in an elegant part of Geneva. Their family name was Finger, which I found enchanting. The Fingers brought me into another world again: a world of softness and tenderness. Their home seemed like warm pudding to me, where their children were coddled like little eggs. Two adorable girls about my age, with hair I could only imagine as a divine gift: sculpted, black curls, *flaschenlocken*, bottle curls as they were called then, that fell, one close to the other, producing movement but not undirected, clearly the kind of curl where human intervention had gently taken place. Another divine gift was luminous, porcelain skin, the signature of young Jewesses in European paintings. Next to them I appeared, at least in my mind, like coarse peasant stock: straight, unruly hair which, on the rare occasions when someone tried to put a curl in it, would deflate within minutes.

'Their house was a soft yellow; the tenderness in their demeanour matched the interior: there was a sense of camaraderie between the house and the people who lived in it. Watching in wonder their bed-time ritual of washing – their mother glided over face and hands with an angel's touch – I saw myself as a waif, given a moment among these story book children. Although they treated me kindly, I sensed that it was pity rather than affection that stirred their hearts.'

As my long lunch with Ruth drew to a close, I sighed: the girls with curls, as I had dubbed them in my writing, had vanished like so many others who had peopled my life nearly sixty years ago. Until this moment, Ruth had been an attentive listener, her talents as an interviewer honed by years of oral history documentation.

'You know, I was at a party a few weeks ago', she began hesitatingly, 'and I met a woman whose name, I think, was Finger. Her father was involved in refugee matters during the war; her name is Michèle Stroun. She's a respected publisher who works in Geneva and Paris. Why don't you call her; you have nothing to lose.'

I was unprepared for the possibility Ruth offered: that I might be reunited with my past in a form other than brittle paper documents (for which I was nevertheless enormously grateful). I had come to accept my refugee fate: that after the war we would be dispersed throughout the world, wherever they would have us; that people we had once loved and to whom we had been attached would disappear; that in all likelihood they would be gone forever from our lives. Could I allow a crack, however delicate, to appear in that stony, resolute apperception?

I was too embarrassed to reveal to Ruth that her perfectly sensible advice struck me as originating from some mythic realm or, closer to our time, from a reunion novel (I have always been drawn to stories that brought together characters from the past, disclosing to the reader how life had turned out for them decades later). Such an ingathering had not been my lot, since we left few traces as we moved from country to country. These residuals of the past left unexpressed, I assured Ruth I would contact Michèle Stroun. 'Nothing to lose', she repeated. Half-heartedly, I placed a call to Metropolis, her publishing office, and was almost relieved to hear that she was not available. Her absence confirmed my expectations. Moreover, I saw it as a sign that I should move on to more realistic efforts.

The march against globalization that was to take place in Geneva on Saturday afternoon had been well publicized in all the media, with hints that it might turn violent. Here was an action I could support, which would not require recapturing the distant past but instead would restore the political activism in which I had been engaged for close to forty years, encompassing the Vietnam war, feminism and other progressive movements. Another reason for being in the heart of Geneva that afternoon was Grand Passage, a large department store which my mother and I used to frequent, although not to shop there; it was really a pretence, a ruse for wheedling boxes from the sales clerks. I don't know why Mama needed all those boxes, but I still picture her entire being animated, coquettishly tilting her head towards her shoulder, arms and hands outstretched, drawing in the air the shape and size of the container she wanted: *'S'il vous plaît, mademoiselle, un petit carton.'*

Grand Passage was also as close as I ever came to tobogganing in Switzerland. During the Christmas season, even in wartime, a giant slide spanning three floors had been installed in the very centre of the store. My mother was not one to let such an event pass without my participation. Terrified though I was, I forced myself to join the jovial Swiss children who seemed born to such an exercise. Almost sixty years later, the same seasonal cheer in place, I wanted to see whether the toboggan had survived the changes in marketing and safety standards, not to mention a litigious population. My hunch was that today's safety regulations would never allow such a dangerous, death-defying roller-coaster ride in the midst of the elegant rows of merchandise.

When I approached Rue du Rhône, where Grand Passage was located and where the march was passing, I saw the police in full gear, only their eyes visible through narrow slits. I longed to join this lively demonstration of adults and children, chanting, singing, tooting their horns, a sight so familiar and welcoming. Fear of arrest in a foreign country kept me on the sidelines, cheering and photographing the event instead. Because of the march, all but one of the entrances to the Grand Passage were closed, to prevent a takeover by this spirited band.

I entered the only open door to the store, which led directly to the book section. Glancing at the titles, all in French, I saw none that was particularly compelling until I came upon *Terres Promises: Avatars du mouvement ouvrier juif au-dela des mers autour de 1900*, by Nathan Weinstock, published by Metropolis; the editor was Michèle Stroun. Turning quickly to the table of contents and the index in this book about the Jewish Labour Movement in North America, Argentina and Palestine, I saw a chapter, 'Toronto la Rouge', and recognized the name of Morris Winshevsky of Canada, and other familiar names. At the back of the volume, in the catalogue extracts, I discovered titles that spoke to me so directly and with such immediacy that I was left gasping for breath. They included feminist writings from France and translations of favourite authors from Hebrew and Yiddish literature, all subjects that have captivated me most of my life.

Serendipity has rarely featured in my life; perhaps my disposition, which leaves little to chance, has discouraged such interventions. This is not self-pity, but rather a sober look at events and circumstances. I have lived my life convinced that if I do not hammer out my existence, nothing of value will emerge. My month in Switzerland in 2001 was the exception: it was as though I had been plucked from the predictable course and gently placed into another being, another persona whose comings and goings were blessed by coincidence and chance. Grand Passage, with only one entrance open, led me to Michèle Stroun's books, as if a literary angel were inscribing me into a land of metaphoric memories.

The concurrence of events was too powerful to ignore; *bashert*, destiny, came to mind. Having the time and space to smoke, to write, to conjecture, kept me from a maelstrom in which I could easily have lost myself. In the journal I kept during my month in Switzerland, I wrote on that afternoon:

> Possible scenarios to consider before placing another phone call to Michèle Stroun:
> She isn't the girl I played with in Geneva so many years ago.
> She can't be reached.
> She is that girl in my past; she listens to my story, wishes me luck in my search, but is too busy to see me.
> She's the one, and she wants to meet.
> Then I indicate shared interests, Yiddish and Feminism. *Found Treasures* (my anthology of Yiddish women writers) comes up.
> Fantasy: we meet, we remember those days and the chemistry between us is good.

Fortified by a glass of beer and cheered on by the young Canadians with whom I was staying, I telephoned. After the first few words in French, we continued in English, and soon ventured into descriptions of the past. Indeed, she was the Finger girl and those were her grandparents who cared for me in 1943. Michèle didn't remember me, but she invited me to coffee on Sunday morning.

Why did it matter so much to have my recollections confirmed? Why do even fleeting memories have so strong a hold on my life? No easy answers come. For refugees, fragmentation marks being in the world, and since so few integral trails remain, any corroboration of solidity is life-giving.

More journal entries:

> *Nov. 11, 2001, Geneva*
> 'C'est vous!' I blurted out as I faced her at the elevator door. The dark, thick hair, the face that speaks, the gesture of welcome accompanied by a quick scrutiny, and finally in that first moment, the jumble of words expressing expectation, anticipation of what

may emerge in the next hours. I've come to Michèle Stroun's apartment in Geneva to relive, retrieve, recover my past, my refugee childhood, my history, and that of my family and other refugees who spent the war years in Switzerland.

Why do these words, 'It is you!', spoken in that instant of recognition, resonate so deeply, so far and so wide, pulling me into the past while holding me fixed in the present moment? In a whirlwind of temporal zones I reel between 1943, when I was a six-year-old, and now, 2001, when I am on a mission to trace and revive those years.

The six-year-old refugee child that I was when I first met Michèle knew only of flight, transition, and temporary shelter.

A kindred spirit found in Michèle Stroun: very warm, *heymish*, lively, generous: a real *mentch* with good politics. A meeting of minds and hearts.

'C'est vous!': I've carried all these years in memory and now you've returned to me as a part of my self. All that happened then was neither fabrication nor post-modern construction. I no longer straddle the dual reality between dream and waking. Actuality matters: feeling your presence, holding you in my gaze, replaces the evanescent with the enduring.

Nov. 13, 2001, on the train to Bern:
I'm afraid to let myself fully experience the joy of being in her presence. That moment of recognition and the ensuing visit are given short shrift here. Why such restraint? Is it because I'm afraid of driving away that moment? It stands out as one of the sweetest moments in my trip; why then not a fullness in bringing it back to life? And the substance of the visit is here merely given headlines. The subsequent dinner with her and her husband I don't even record. I will have to return.

These ruminations accompanied me everywhere I went that month in Switzerland. So often during that month I would try to squeeze the past back into present consciousness by trickery, or studied concentration, all in the hopes of assurance that my life was lived in time and place, not merely in my mind and imagination. Was it the internalization of the age-old Jewish injunction to remember? Did I perceive it my obligation to be a witness, to inscribe a true and accurate account of this particular aspect into the annals of the Holocaust, which, given my age and experience, I could render?

4

MORGINS: THE ALPINE SHTETL AUGUST 1943–OCTOBER 1945

1943

The Jews of Europe
9 February: Deportations from France to Auschwitz-Birkenau and Sobibor resume.
19 April: Liquidation of Warsaw ghetto with ensuing revolt.
30 April: Establishment of the Bergen-Belsen 'exchange camp', later a concentration camp.
11 June: Himmler orders the liquidation of all existing ghettos in Eastern Europe.
2 August: Revolt of prisoners in Treblinka extermination camp.
16 September: Deportation of Jews from northern Italy to Auschwitz-Birkenau begins.
1–2 October: Arrest of Jews in Denmark begins; resistance by population and officials prevents systematic deportation.
1 October: Revolt of prisoners in Sobibor extermination camp.

International Events
19–30 April: Anglo-American Bermuda Conference on the refugee question.
13 October: Italy proclaims war on Germany.
9 November: Founding of the United Nations Relief and Rehabilitation Administration (UNRRA).

Swiss Refugee Policy
1 March: The Federal Council Decree on Housing for Refugees centralizes authority with the federal government, orders the internment of all refugees accepted since August 1942, and places their assets under the administration of the EJPD.
26 July: EJPD directives ease conditions for entering Switzerland.
27 July: EJPD directive concerning the southern border orders the expulsion of all illegal refugees to Italy.
17 September: According to EJPD directives, the flow of refugees from

Italy is so large that male refugees over 16 are to be turned away. September–December: Switzerland takes in some 20,000 members of the military and 7,800 civilian refugees from Italy.

(Informamation from Independent Commission of Experts Switzerland – Second World War, Jean-François Bergier, Chairman, *Switzerland and Refugees in the Nazi Era.*)

In the restless movement between childhood memory and documented life, I favoured memory, a palimpsest of tender images with few layers of lasting unhappiness. Archival records have forced me to look more closely at my glossy picture of the past. Friends also have cast doubt on my depictions of an idyllic refugee childhood: 'You must have felt some dislocation, some sense of loss', they've prodded. I have re-entered Morgins, the centrepiece of my Swiss years, to uncover truths left untold and realized only through painful acts of restoration. An overlay of innocence, of simplicity, concealed a maze of feelings; I questioned my right to portray those years as deprivation. Compared to Jewish children in the rest of Europe, in concentration camps or in hiding, my daily life was paradisiacal and my woes trivial. And yet there is a truth I cling to in the act of describing my good fortune, safe in Switzerland during the Holocaust. I search for words to carry the moral complexity I inhabit and the actuality I want to convey in the intermingling of injury and felicity.

Because luck is random, amoral, I assert its presence; I know that during the war years, acumen or foresight was not the determining factor for survival. One day a guard might have looked aside and let a band of fleeing Jews cross into Switzerland; another day, another guard would not let them pass or, worse, turn them over to the Germans. Swiss refugee policy also changed from week to week, reflecting public and media responses to the draconian measures against Jews who could not enter as political refugees because racial laws did not apply. Yet basking in one's good fortune in the midst of evil is immoral. To be faithful to my past, to bring it into the open, to allow events and experience to unfold without restraint, to reveal this seldom told story, I had to bracket these prescriptive categories that weighed so heavily.

Not trusting to memory alone, I consulted numerous sources to find links to my past, including organization archives, historical accounts and memoirs. Although these general resources were helpful in providing background, the particulars were still missing. In June 1999, while in New York caring for my newborn granddaughter, my cousin Fritzi, whose hand I'd clutched while crossing the border, telephoned me with astonishing news. The files of former refugees in Switzerland, the official documentation of their stay, were now accessible; all that was needed to receive them was a written request. Chaotic, unsettling thoughts rushed in: after a fifty-year hiatus, my family's records still existed somewhere; vital signs, clues to my childhood were buried in some tomb in Switzerland.

Six weeks later, a securely wrapped package arrived from the Swiss Federal Archives: 150 pages of photocopied documents. I perused the pages with their faded official stamps from various Swiss cantons and police bureaucracies: some were spread before me on my small table, others had slipped to the floor. The accompanying letter read:

> Refugees Files of the Johles Family
>
> Dear Mrs. Forman,
>
> In response to your letter from June 9, we can inform you that there is a file existing in the records of the Eidgenoessissische Polizeiabteilung (Federal Division of Police) at our archives about Max Johles, Malka Johles-Komornik and Frieda and Kasiel Aba Johles under the archives code E4264 1985/196 N 4930. You will find enclosed copies and a microfilm of your family's file without charge.
>
> We hope that the document contains some interesting information about your family's stay during World War II in Switzerland.
>
> Sincerely yours,
>
> SWISS FEDERAL ARCHIVES: Reading Room Section,
> Dr D. Bourgeois/H. Von Ruette.

I see my parents' signatures, so precise a revelation of their inner life: my father's regular script, lightly adorned but clear and steady; my mother's ornate, chaotic script, hard to decipher in our age of devalued penmanship. Their presence is embodied in these layers of applications – for Mama's medical leave, for Papa's special request to spend Passover with his family, for renewal permits whilst we await our visas for immigration to America – and in detailed questionnaires, including autobiographical entries, and the minutiae of financial accounts. I look to these half-century-old refugee files to lead me back to the child I was, a child whose life was determined and controlled by the testimonies now in front of me. My own small file, number 4930, includes a photograph: in it I look bewildered yet present, the signature ribbon of those years oddly fixed in my hair. My return is full of doubt. Why retrace these steps and risk the disruption the past will certainly provoke? Fleetingimages vie with administrative records whose faded, much-stamped pages provide answers to puzzling events and fill gaps in my memory.

In my family file is a letter received by my parents on 17 August 1943: in Germanic tone and language, I find their orders to leave Geneva. Papa was to report to the train station at 6.30 a.m., four days hence, to be taken to a work camp in Sierre. Mama received an identical letter, but her destination was the family internment camp in Morgins. My name did not appear in either directive, but since my mother's destination was a family camp, I was included in her journey. My 16-year-old brother Max had by this time been integrated into the Youth Aliyah Home in Versoix, a suburb of Geneva; it was a *hakhsharah*, a Zionist camp preparing him for post-war settlement in Palestine.

Mama and I arrived in Morgins on 21 August. The journey, only forty-seven miles from Geneva but involving two train changes and a spiralling bus ride, took the greater part of a day and brought with it major changes in landscape. Geneva, that vibrant city with its open, bustling streets, lavish parks and playgrounds, numerous varied shops and large central railway station – all these gave way to this tiny village. Geography now complied with policy: we were enclosed and our lives would be lived in that tight little valley for two years, but of course we children had no idea how long we would be there.

On that day in August, my father was abruptly taken from my mother and me; he would be absent from our lives for the next nine months. On that same day, I was thrust into a communal existence with other refugee children. No longer did I experience the centrality that was unquestionably mine as the cherished and cosseted child of two middle-aged parents. I was unprepared; my throne toppled; I was now one among many.

At an altitude of 1,400 metres, just where the Valaisian Alps begin, lies the village of Morgins. For over a century it has drawn tourists to its mineral waters, mountains and forests. Before the war, it had been a winter resort, renowned for its ski trails and toboggan runs, a favourite of British tourists. In 1943, with tourism on the decline, a more modest constituency was brought to this former playground of the rich: it was assigned to more than 400 Jewish women, men and children from every occupied country in Europe. The native Swiss, receding unobtrusively into the background, seemed almost to disappear as the refugees with their unruly children took over this bucolic Eden.

The mountains were dotted with peaceful cows, the echoes of bells a constant reminder of their presence. Since we were internees, not colonizers, it is perhaps hyperbolic to speak of a takeover, but the sheer tumult, tension and nervousness of the refugees filled this once peaceful terrain, obscuring its past.

In my recollections, Morgins is permanently dominated by 'our hill', a gravel corridor linking the adult residence, Le Grand Hôtel, at the base of the hill, to the youth hostel at the top, where the children were housed. Close by there was a pond, and just beyond it we saw the French border, a wooded path we never crossed; we knew that over there, in France, the war was going on. Built in nineteenth-century opulence, the Grand Hotel's commodious lobby was lined with plush, red velvet sofas; these would, in the course of two years, be eviscerated by the refugee children. Undisturbed by the surrounding destruction of property, their mothers did not drop a stitch in their knitting nor the thread of their conversation; that image of quiet subversion and resistance I still hold dear today.

Within sight of the Grand Hotel was the bus station, the hub of Morgins, where life swirled as in a Breughel painting; there a much-coveted leave to the city began and ended. At that crossroads, amongst other anxious and impatient refugees, I would await my father's arrival. After nine months in the Sierre work camp, Papa was granted a transfer to Morgins. Occasionally he was allowed a trip to Geneva, a centre of Jewish welfare activity. As I watched the travellers descending from the bus, I had eyes only for him, confident that he would always have a gift for me: once, a red leather heart-shaped coin purse, and from another trip a pair of cobalt-blue sunglasses. How did he know what I would delight in for years to come? I kept the cherished coin purse until I passed it on to my daughter when she was old enough to appreciate its value.

My family's file of archival documents, as well as the 1999 Bergier Report, *Switzerland and Refugees in the Nazi Era*, all complement and compete with my own recollections of the four years spent there. Within these shifting temporal zones lie my doubts: how to prevent these years from being absorbed by the sheer volume and weight of the past. I close my eyes in the hope of retrieving these dream-like years, of re-entering the body of the child I was: to once again feel the cold of the Alpine winters and the itchy wool pants my mother knitted so laboriously. I long to re-enter the body of the child who walked through the fir forest of Morgins in search of berries, who never tired of braiding daisy chains: the child who one morning saw a giant riding toward her on a horse – the doctor who would remove her tonsils in the village clinic.

I lived in Morgins from August 1943 to October 1945. These two elastic years sometimes seem an endless stretch, but at other times a compressed world that releases a rush of memories when touched. The very name Morgins evokes a spectrum of scenes as in a montage; gradually the performers enter, they/we/I are all actors. Recreating those scenes, I am at times the audience – looking, searching, watching – and then I'm on stage, not always central but present in some role. Memory, my guide, the *passeur*, leads me back and forth, sometimes closer to the event and place, other times further away, so that they become dim, or merely outlines. Every scene in that geography of emotions is peopled and heavily laden. I conjure up images of an isolated, insular kingdom of children, where magic and misery were intertwined, where time stood still. For over half a century, Morgins remained a place, a time, an enclosed capsule, which I could enter at will.

Morgins conferred on us the status of internees; with that camp came the respite of internment, the resignation to our fate. These words can be spoken without the shudder that usually attends such a description because, safe and sheltered, we were free to be merely interned, merely restricted. With the exception of my father's absence of nine months, I was seldom separated from my parents. The daily closeness to them allowed a semblance of normal life. Moreover, they were doting and indulgent parents whose love protected me from the harsher conditions of refugee life. In Morgins I found security and even contentment.

The information in the Johles file confirms Papa's absence and explains why Mama shared a room with a rabbi's wife, whom I knew only by her honorific title, *Rebbetzin*. In all likelihood her husband was in another camp or, worse, had been deported, and she was now alone. As a rabbi's wife she carried a mantle of honour and prestige. In normal times she and my mother would not have been in the same social circle and would certainly not have shared the intimacy of a bedroom. She was older than my mother and I don't recall ever seeing her with a child at her side.

My father's internment in Sierre left Mama and me in similar positions: we were both displaced from our former quarters, she now in her dormitory with the *Rebbetzin* and I in mine with the children. It was a time when I was beginning to make many discoveries about people, their dispositions and personalities, and this began with the

Rebbetzin, who remains alive in my memory although she and Mama were room-mates for less than a year.

My first visit to the adult dormitory, my mother's bright and spacious room, threw me into a state of confusion. Mama had a favourite phrase she used to describe disorder, '*vi bay der rebetsin in bet*' (like in the *Rebbetzin*'s bed). That picture of an unmade bed, sheets and blankets twisted, became my way of comprehending clutter. As I entered their room that day, I saw the *Rebbetzin* sitting on her immaculate, neatly-made bed. I was bewildered; what was going on here?

'Mama', I said, 'you always told me that a *Rebbetzin*'s bed was a mess. Her bed is so neat.' A sheepish smile concealed my mother's embarrassment, but the *Rebbetzin* laughed heartily and I felt an immediate bond with her.

The *Rebbetzin* wore a close-fitting golden brown *sheitel*, the traditional wig of Orthodox Jewish women, which I had never seen before. She exuded calm, an aura of dignity and decorum evident in her movement and bearing, and I sensed that she was from another sphere compared to most of the women I saw in the camp. My attachment to the *Rebbetzin* grew during those months. She almost took my father's place, in Mama's room as well as in his customary role as the comforter in my life. One instance stands out in my memory: I had scraped my knee rather badly, an open, bleeding wound calling for attention. Mama tried to wash it, but I wouldn't let her near me. I ran from her, screaming with pain and fear; I was out of control. At that moment, the *Rebbetzin* entered the room. Without a word, she approached me, gently extending her hand to me. I stopped my dervish-like movements. She crooned, '*Kum aher zis maydele, hob nit moyre*' (Come here sweet girl, don't be afraid). Quietly she explained why the wound needed washing and how, with a clean bandage, healing would take place and the pain would soon be gone. She spoke to me just as Papa would have.

My relationship to the *Rebbetzin* also introduced layers of doubt into my world: how could my mother have been so wrong in her stereotyping? Our *Rebbetzin* was nothing like Mama's depiction. In fact, she was her opposite, a sharp contrast. Little coherence came from Mama, who was never in one place mentally, so often in the past or in the continuous present, a present that drew mysteriously from an unspoken past. Reading James Joyce as an adult was a return to a language I'd always known; I'd grown up with these streams of consciousness.

My family's treasured documents from the Swiss Archives authenticate a lived life, but they also intrude into a world that I've carried with me, as if packed in a suitcase, for over half a century. I move back and forth between, on one hand, the urgency to reveal, to open the files, to give them new life and new translation, and on the other hand, hesitation, misgivings about my capacity to do justice to this moment in history where my own experience remains. How do I correlate the larger, tragic history of that period with my own quotidian reality as a refugee child, exposed to, yet sheltered from, full knowledge of the events beyond Switzerland? In a setting enclosed by mountains, protected by parents and teachers, I also confront those acts of childhood that are both singular and universal.

Deprived of traditional family life, we children were forced to define our social world in the camp without the reassurance or intimate guidance of parents, grandparents or other relatives. The camp provided protection from the enemy who would destroy us, but could not offer us the luxury of gradual introduction to the ways of friendship and relationships. Thrust into a world of strangers, albeit from the same genetic pool, we had to muddle through, to discover or create on our own the tools and tokens for acceptance among our peers. Modelled on the kibbutz, Morgins placed children and parents in separate spheres; we found little refuge within our families who were seldom available for mediation or intervention.

Before Mama and I came to Morgins, I'd had little formal exposure to other children. Now I was always part of a group: sleeping, eating, hiking and playing. Alone only in my mind – perhaps not even there. Did I ever think of myself as an individual or only as part of a crowd? I've used every device I know to bring back friends, playmates, peers who shared my life. I've beckoned to them in scenes I've conjured up: the classroom, dormitory, dining hall, the forest and mountains. I have hoped and waited for them to present themselves to me again, sixty years later, stories in hand ready to be immortalized. But when they do appear in memory, they are an unmanageable lot; they do not line up in an orderly fashion. Instead, a few push to the front of the line demanding their time on stage, while others remain in the background, part of the scenery.

The friendships I recall most vividly are those that bring with them moral dilemmas and lessons, very much like the fables of La Fontaine that were part of the literature in my early years. Perhaps it was his name, which spoke so directly of friendship, that places Ami in a stellar position in my recollections of childhood society. We loved each other with the simplicity and innocence of 6-year-olds. Our days were spent together in class, at mealtimes, mountain climbing, berry picking and other communal activities.

A pretty boy with a lively, wide-eyed look on the world and a sweet disposition, he was much loved by our counsellors as well as by the other children. I don't recall a mother, and her absence may have accounted for the obvious affection shown to him by the adults in the camp. I was made of rougher material – on the dishevelled side, hair always undone, clothes ill-fitting, frequent bouts of impetigo. I looked like a refugee child, while Ami appeared to have been dropped there by accident.

The children's house included our dormitories, eight iron beds to a room with few adornments. Boys slept on the second floor, girls on the third. Every night, one of the mothers was on watch, soothing the restless, trying to catch the bed-wetters (an epidemic among refugee children) before it was too late. One evening, I came to Ami's room as he was preparing for bed. I wanted to say 'Good night', kiss him and tuck him in. I stood by his bed; I didn't want to let him go, from my sight, from my hold.

Out of nowhere, from some unreachable height, I heard his father: '*Qu'est-ce que tu fais ici?*' (What are you doing in the boys' room?) A voice of controlled rage and authority: 'Don't ever come here again!' Ami's father always wore a navy-blue beret, appropriate for a Frenchman, but in the camp, where most of the men wore skullcaps, he stood out. His posture was erect, almost arrogant, at a time when so many were bent with grief. He was conspicuous, too, because he was one of the few native French-speakers in a country and setting where that language was prized.

Bewildered, humiliated, I fled to my room. What had I done to evoke such a harsh sentence? In my bed that night I tried to piece it all together. Hadn't the mother on night duty in the boys' room smiled at my motherly act? She'd shown no disapproval of my presence there. What did Ami's father know about me that she hadn't suspected? I began to think that Ami's father could look into my heart and see what I could not.

The next morning at breakfast, Ami was somewhat less exuberant than usual. He told me with little affect that his father didn't want me to come to his room again. I said nothing. Soon after, Ami and his father left the camp, and I never saw them again.

Some years later, when I heard the story of Adam and Eve – God's exposure of their sin, their shame at their nakedness – I recalled Ami's father, his god-like appearance and warning. Or had I already known of Eve's sin when my nocturnal visit was exposed, assuming her guilt to be my heritage and Ami's father's voice to be the voice of God? I'll never know which came first, but that episode brought love, fear and hate as close together as they would ever be for me.

I recall the attachment, dear to my heart but fraught with self-doubt, to my best friend Sorale, Rabbi Klein's daughter. The rabbi was one of our teachers, a gentle, soft-spoken man, serious about his vocation. One day Sorale misbehaved in class and her father ordered her to stand in the corner. We, her classmates, were to wag a shaming finger at her. I didn't want to be on the side of her tormentors; we had a tender friendship and I knew that this was not how friends behaved towards one another. I see her standing in the corner of our sunlit classroom, a long-limbed girl with delicate features and soft, curled hair. She stands cowed, taking shelter from a downpour of pointing fingers.

Did I follow the others in meting out her punishment or did I resist her father's orders and take a courageous stand in support of my friend? I do not recall my stance, but I cannot forget the conflict I felt between obedience to authority and loyalty to friendship. To this day, ethical questions of compliance, power, domination and betrayal preoccupy my thoughts and actions.

As our time in Morgins passed, predictable patterns emerged – predictable because even in this extraordinary setting, cliques existed, and those children who in normal life would have been leaders assumed that position here. I frequently found myself on the periphery of the girls' coterie, quite possibly because of my rumpled appearance and tomboyish personality. Such distinctions were rigidly in place in the Europe of the 1940s, and it was in the boys' social constellation that I found easy acceptance and companionship. As a feminist, I'm now embarrassed to confess that I found the boys more fun, more adventurous and amusing than my own little sisterhood. Boys represented ease in the world; they conveyed an air of being freer and less encumbered by conventions of dress and behaviour. They were true and steadfast. In the company of girls, I was in, then out, never sure how long the period of grace would last, how long I would be accepted as one of them. My association with the boys did not go unnoticed, nor was it without its own brand of conflict. A boy outside our inner circle taunted me, calling me 'their wife'. I felt sinful, but at the same time I was glad that in their eyes I belonged.

In November 2001, on a research fellowship, I extended my project beyond family files and beyond memories – my own and those of former refugees whom I interviewed in Toronto and New York. The grant allowed me to immerse myself at the source, the foundation, bedrock, as my son Gideon, the philosophy student, expounded when he learned of my forthcoming trip to examine archival holdings and material resources, and to revisit the places of my past.

I knew beforehand that the Zurich archives, the major repository of Swiss Jewish documentation, would yield useful information, yet I was unprepared for the riches that came my way. Once the archivists at the Archiv für Zeitgeschichte in Zurich were familiar with my research project, they joined the expedition with the open-heartedness and enthusiasm I would expect only of old friends. They delivered file boxes containing records of correspondence, reports and meeting agendas of Jewish welfare organizations, along with the papers of Swiss relief associations. Over the weeks I was there, my crowded work-table became a centre of transformation, from officialdom to the daily life of refugees. Individual narratives were yet to come.

One morning, Claudia Hoerschelmann, a senior archivist and historian of Second World War refugees in Switzerland, who was guiding my research, urged me to move beyond documents. She maintained that only by interviewing people who had been engaged in wartime activities with refugees would I find what I was seeking, the 'flesh and blood' of refugee experience (a rather ghoulish term for this particular population, I thought). I protested that every piece of paper was animated, spoke to me and revealed its own life and story. However, my passionate appeal did not convince her; in her view, I needed further persuasion.

Later that morning, as though continuing our conversation, Claudia delicately placed on my desk a file box containing a collection of refugee children's drawings. They had been part of an exhibition accompanying an international study week on 'the war-damaged child', held in Zurich during September 1945. She explained that the Central Directorate for Homes and Camps had been perceived as commanding camp life in a militaristic manner, and after the war faced an 'image-problem'. The exhibition of children's drawings was an opportunity for a softer, more caring model to emerge. Samuel Jean-Richard, who had organized the exhibition back in 1945, lived near Zurich. If I wished, she would initiate the contact and leave the details for a meeting to me.

As in a well-choreographed performance, where every step contributes to the whole, another archivist presented herself, holding close to her chest what looked like an art book. How lovely, I thought, they want to introduce some diversion into my rigorous work. At first glance, all I saw was the multicoloured cover with a child's stick drawing and text below. With few words of explanation, the archivist slipped away, leaving me with the lavishly illustrated book, *Kinderbilderwelten: Zeichnungen von Flüchtlingskindern 1945* (*The Worlds of Children's Pictures: Drawings by Refugee Children 1945*). My eyes darted back and forth between the original drawings on the table before me and the book published earlier that year (2001) in Zurich. The book blends drawings, biographical data and a brief psychological evaluation of over seventy children who spent the war years in Switzerland. In his introduction, the editor, Andreas Renold, states that all the children who participated in the drawing exercise had been interned in camps; all were there at least with their mothers, some with both parents. I turned to the index to see which camps were included in the exhibit. Morgins was there.

Later that same day, true to her word, Claudia related with restrained pleasure that the ground had been prepared and Samuel Jean-Richard was expecting my call. I telephoned and asked to meet with him at his home, but he insisted on coming to the archives, an hour's train ride from Zurich. I knew that he was close to 90 years old, and I expected to see a feeble man carrying those years. Instead, a vigorous personage appeared the next day, looking more like 60: upright posture, long hair, one earring, a leather shoulder bag and an elegant hippie coat.

During the war, the Central Committee for Camps and Homes assigned the task of establishing the first refugee camp for families in St Cierge to Jean-Richard, an art teacher by profession. He became its first head and was later promoted to inspector of camps with responsibility for schooling, vocational education and recreation for children and youth.

Our talk in the small archive cafeteria was amiable and animated; by this time I'd lost my inhibition about speaking German. It was altogether a meeting without mediation; for that instant we were just two people in the universe speaking to each other. He remembered everything and everyone from those days: my little friend Sorale, who with her family was transferred from St Cierge to Morgins; Sorale's father, Rabbi Klein, one of my favourite teachers, who presented Jean-Richard with a *Sefer Torah* as a farewell tribute when he left St Cierge. Jean-Richard returned it, he told me, because what was a holy scroll for the camp refugees held only folkloric value for him.

It was getting late. I knew he had a lengthy commute to his home, but I delayed our farewells as long as my conscience allowed. Enraptured by every detail of his chronicle, I sensed that for him, too, this was a journey he did not want to end. Finally, as I was packing up my tape recorder, my head spinning from the day's revelations, Jean-Richard casually asked whether I remembered having drawn pictures for the exhibition in 1945. I replied that I had no recollection of the event itself, but that I had seen the book of drawings. I added, with only a hint of disappointment in my voice, that none of the pictures was mine. We parted as friends. I was elated at having met this man from the past, this raconteur who returned a part of my life to me.

By 9.15 the following morning I was back at the archives, eager to tell the staff about the previous day's encounter. Before I could utter a word, a young archivist greeted me excitedly with the news that Samuel Jean-Richard had already phoned and given them the identifying file number for my drawings – #677.

Here they are. I see them, 'Frieda Johles, 7 *Ans*' clearly written at the top, fresh, undamaged by fifty-seven years in storage: two pictures, a self-portrait and a house with a picket fence, bordered by flowers and a bare tree. Within minutes, one of the technicians produces an excellent photocopy for me. The house drawing is very tidy, colourful, and I am instantly reminded of how meticulously I used to depict roof shapes by little overlapping half circles. The drawing of the house exudes serenity.

Weeks later, when I recounted the discovery of these drawings to my daughter Jessica, a psychologist and art therapist, I mused, 'It reads like the home of a child growing up in a peaceful suburb.' Professional as well as daughter, she listened to my presentation, examined the evidence, and cautioned, 'Not so fast, Mum. Do you see that bare tree by the side of the house? That is not a sign of contentment, nor of well-being. Morgins was not your suburban home on Long Island.' Tenacious as always, she pointed to a darkened window, which in my enthusiasm I had overlooked, and gently concluded the analysis of her mother's childhood drawing. 'That window on the ground floor, pencilled in black, next to a clear window, certainly indicates ambivalence, hiding and exposing; you weren't sure.' That sobering diagnosis uncovered yet another layer in what was to become a journey of demystification.

The self-portrait, which even I could perceive was closer to the actuality of that time, reveals a wildness, eyes gazing outward at the world. In the accompanying text, a camp teacher described me as 'A very lively child, often outspoken'. An attentive archivist explained that in 1945, *vorlaut*, outspoken, signalled veiled criticism, while today it would be regarded as a desirable trait, 'every parent's wish'. So, even then, I was outspoken. My German dictionary defines the word as 'pert', as 'giving tongue too soon'. I like that allusion to tongue given too soon: it fits so well with what I often see in myself as I blurt out something daring, perhaps better left unsaid.

My return to Toronto became a series of occasions to relive the month of revelation and disclosure in Switzerland. Friends and family who saw my drawings and heard my stories responded emotionally, often with tears. They scrutinized my expression; they asked how I felt when the drawings were first shown to me at the archives.

'I stumbled over my words, I was in turmoil', I answered. 'I still haven't fully grasped their significance, I'm holding back from embracing this portrait of myself as a 7-year-old, I look at the drawings fondly but from a distance.'

Why, I ask myself, was I unable to experience the reality of that moment when my drawings were presented to me? Why did I pack away that first sight of them, placing them in an already overstuffed suitcase of moments to be examined at a later time? I stood there in the foyer of the archives, surrounded by strangers whose reception of my discovery was more impassioned than mine. Was that stoic posture yet another manifestation of a refugee: watchful, fearful that I might lose control in front of others, that the tears welling up would turn from tender moisture to an unstoppable torrent? So often in my life I have longed for tears that will not come.

I find also the drawings produced by my little gang of Morgins children: Ruth, Michel, David and Hannah who was my competitor and adversary during the years of internment. My playmates' drawings appear as miracles: to recover their pictures, after all these years. This is yet another aspect of the research trip that is so beyond anything I could have predicted. First in Zurich and now back in Toronto, it all has a dream-like quality or even the quality of a children's fairy tale: the little girl finds her friends again after many years and they are reunited. Hannah was described in the last sentence of the questionnaire as a precocious child, outspoken, vain, 'peacocky'. It is uncanny and yet oddly reassuring to discover, after half a century's passing, that my impression of her then, and in subsequent years when I wrote about her, coincides with the written evaluation by her camp teacher. Two years older than I, she was my nemesis during the years of internment in Morgins; the age difference alone did not fully explain her position of leadership among the children. Our standing in the community was determined not only by who we were but also by family attachments. My mother, unconventional and eccentric in behaviour and appearance, placed me on shaky ground, while Hannah's mother, composed and self-contained, walked through the camp as if she were still in pre-war Berlin, as if nothing had changed.

Shortly before we all left Morgins I was to witness a different and darker aspect of Hannah's mother. It remains in my mind as a night of violence. Walking up the stairs to our dormitory I saw her beating and kicking Hannah, who had collapsed on the floor. I sensed that this was no ordinary spanking such as I had on occasion observed, but an uncontrolled episode. Later that evening, Hannah sobbed about the incident to her father as he sat by her bed, tenderly stroking her hair. In my continuing education in matters of the human condition, I learned that the inner and outer do not always correspond.

Many of the commentaries on the boys' drawings stated that they were 'badly brought up, spoiled by their mothers, in need of a father's hand'. The missing father's hand reminded me that not all children in the camp were blessed with both parents present: some fathers had been deported and murdered, others had escaped to havens in Europe and abroad, and still others had disappeared without a trace. As I read these harsh judgements about my lovable little friends' deportment and manners and their mothers' failures as disciplinarians, I am struck once again by the enormous disparity between the worlds of the refugees and their Swiss caregivers. Although my behaviour was not deemed as offensive as that of the boys, I nevertheless include myself in these characterizations. I too was mischievous, strong-willed and undisciplined. Today, I rejoice that we were not cowed by expectations of compliance and gratitude, that we maintained our self-respect in the only way we could: by being children.

The book of drawings holds so many clues to who I was, who my friends were, how we were perceived by psychologists meeting to discuss war-damaged children. The exhibit was installed in the Federal University of Technology in Zurich, a complex of university buildings that houses the modern history archives where I was sitting at that moment. No longer do I exist in mind and memory alone; I now belong to a category, established by professionals, which I approach with some trepidation but also with great inquisitiveness: what will I discover about myself that I missed in my own efforts at self-recovery? What else will I remember? That same curiosity we carry through a lifetime when we wonder: what do they think of me? I've moved from one abstraction, 'refugee child', to a more specific but still generalized category of 'war-damaged', with implications for the present. Drawings and evaluations by a camp teacher allow the formulation to recede and my own complexities to emerge. I was more than just a war-injured, refugee child, one label stuck onto another; I was also a lively outspoken child.

Psychologists then and now agree that early trauma contributes to lifelong neuroses, to psychological problems; the clinicians' eyes, fixed on me, brand me for life. I, who for so many years wanted only to obliterate all traces of my refugee identity, to distance myself from that past, have come to embrace all labels, including stigmatizing categories. As a 9-year-old, a newcomer to America, I was desperate to erase the blot of 'refugee child'. Now, more than six decades later, I zealously seek out all identifying sources and signs of those years in Switzerland.

During the war years, every issue of *Israelitisches Wochenblatt* was dominated by accounts of refugee life. Week after week, extensive articles on the plight of refugees filled its pages, covering restrictions at the borders, conditions in the camps, political, public and community debates and all matters touching Jewish life during the war. Examining the publication on microfiche and later in photocopies, I was able to look into daily life among my co-religionists throughout Switzerland. The weekly column '*Aus den Lagern*' (From the Camps) featured the comings and goings of individual camps: their cultural programmes and religious observances, along with their trials and tribulations. On 8 October 1943, the following item appeared in *Israelitisches Wochenblatt*:

> A long awaited wish has been realized: a women's and children's internment home with a Kosher kitchen is now in Morgins. The camp administrator, Herr Gruender, is making the greatest effort also to create a model home. The kindergarten in particular is well organized and directed in authentic Jewish tradition by gifted Jewish young ladies like Freulein Ostersetzer, Theresia Kornfeld and others. The director of the kindergarten is Frau Sas.

The newspaper description of well-organized classes, just a few weeks after the camp's establishment, and its suggestion of a systematized kindergarten programme, differs somewhat from my own recollections. Our schooling came closer to the ideals of contemporary 'free schools'. My own children's alternative schools encouraged that spirit of unfettered learning, where curiosity and discovery were allowed free rein. Our camp 'free school' was probably more the result of benign neglect rather than pedagogic principles.

Two weeks later, our new home was once again cited in '*Aus den Lagern*':

> Free time is well spent by the youth in Morgins. In addition to language courses and professional training, free time is for the most part given over to Jewish studies, thereby maintaining the essentials of this community's spirit ... In the Kindergarten of Camp Morgins, fifty children are cared for in the best Jewish tradition. This effort is greatly appreciated by the camp administrator, who summed up his words of praise for the youthful achievements with the maxim: 'We learn from our sorrows.'

I came upon similar references to Morgins in the 21 January 1944 issue:

> Spiritual and intellectual life is flourishing in the internment camp of Morgins. During this period of compulsory stay in the camp they take great pains to use the time for spiritual and intellectual benefit. Thus, a Beth Jacob School has been in place there for some time. As in all Beth Jacob schools, 'Jewish daughters' are instructed in Judaic studies such as the Bible, history, etc. In this way they are educated to be conscious Jews, and may eventually become instructors or kindergarten teachers. For men, study sessions are organized such as Talmud or Bible. Additionally, every Friday evening (Sabbath Eve) a resident presents a lecture on the weekly Torah portion; at least once a week a lecture is given for the entire population. Thus, on January 12th, renowned artist Simcha Schwartz, the director of a theatre group here, began his series of talks with an evening of literary humour; he dedicated the evening to works by Sholom Aleichem. Simcha Schwartz performed very artfully and provided the residents [with] a pleasant diversion. Last but not least, under the leadership of Mr Schuss, regular meetings are held to deal with Jewish and general problems.

The Beth Jacob School for Girls continued to gain attention in *Israelitisches Wochenblatt* on 16 June 1944:

> Since January there exists in Morgins a Beth Jacob School, whose assignment is the training of Jewish instructors and kindergarten teachers. Begun with modest resources, very satisfactory results have already been achieved. Rabbi Dr

> Ehrmann who recently examined the students expressed his pleasure. A number of students are simultaneously teachers in the camp kindergarten and thus have the opportunity of integrating theory with practice.

More evidence of Morgins' status as a creditable school comes in a memo of November 1944, issued by the Central Work Camp division (EJPD), ordering the registration of all camp children who have reached the compulsory school age of 7. Only Morgins is exempted: 'But the Orthodox children in Morgins are not affected; seven year olds will continue, as in the past, to be schooled in the camp itself.'

Eagerly, I include myself in that collectivity of Morgins children: it is my kindergarten, my daily life that is being noted and inscribed in Jewish history. I am part of that fragment of Holocaust testimony. The emphasis on the Jewish aspect of our schooling adds a richer, more textured dimension. Our days were infused by Jewishness; the subjects we learned, the songs we sang, the holidays we celebrated all came from the same source. Remembrances of those profound influences on my early years, which have informed all subsequent days of my life, are enriched by my discovery of journalistic entries such as the one of 17 March 1944:

> On regular workdays there is nothing to distinguish the internment camp in Morgins from other camps: men in overalls, women and girls in aprons. Even meals are almost the same, instead of meat, there is fish. But come the Sabbath or Jewish holidays, then we know immediately that we are in a 'Kosher home'. Everyone in Sabbath clothing, a *Yom Tov* [holiday] mood takes over. So, too, on this Purim. First, a puppet show, presented by director Simche Schwartz, then the children put on a Purim theatre piece. In the evening a variety show to bring the Morginers into a Purim mood, followed by a male choir under the direction of Cantor Wyntraub. On the week-end, Morgins had a guest, Cantor S. Engelmeier.

Because Morgins was an Orthodox camp, our education was all-embracing. Learning and living were integrated into a universe that was purposeful, cognizant of its mission, and intensely conscious of history and our present condition. A tent of *Yiddishkeyt* spread over us in what we saw and heard: *yarmulkes* or *sheitels* on heads, Yiddish on the tongue (Yiddish was the lingua franca of the adults, of the children, *la langue Française*). In countless ways, Morgins resembled the shtetls of our grandparents and parents in their youth. Like the original, Morgins was not a monolith: some of the refugees were more observant than others but all inhabited a deeply Jewish village in the Alps.

From time to time, when my inner voice grows silent, I interrupt the recollections and recording of my days in Morgins by turning to documents. Some are personal, others are organizational and official and still others are public, such as the Swiss Jewish weekly. I leave my memories when I sense that I have omitted the larger world or when I want to compare my impressions with another source. Written from a deeply felt community identity, *Israelitisches Wochenblatt* brings me that much needed breath from the outside, like a strong wind passing through. I feel myself in the company of others, to whom I can pose questions which may be answered, or bring new concerns to the fore.

What were the events in Morgins that touched my parents' lives? The regular presence of Morgins in the '*Lager*' column allows me a glimpse into weekly events of which I was largely unaware, or that have been forgotten in the intervening years. I examine the pages listing an evening's events – a speaker, a concert, a theatre piece; the column also includes extended projects, programmes lasting months, all part of adult life in Morgins. I feel that I'm peeking into my parents' lives, seeing for the first time their daily experience, discovering that they had a life apart from their role as my benefactors and protectors. I move away from the haven of memory where I arrange every aspect, every beginning and end, every boundary and opening, whom I let in and whom I exclude. I relinquish a court where I reign supreme and allow another reality, an objective and contingent world to enter. To consider the proceedings before me, which include my parents, I have to abandon the safety of solipsism, the inner order, and acknowledge this claim on my thoughts.

While I now know of the goings-on in Morgins, I still don't know whether my parents participated in any of the many and varied activities provided during 'free time'. Did they attend concerts? They were not musical, although Papa loved a good cantor and would have enjoyed an evening of liturgical music. Neither then nor in later years did I ever hear them refer to a cultural event in the camp. I presume they would have gone to hear the various speakers who came to Morgins because later, as new immigrants in Boston, they were faithful attenders of lectures to which I too was taken.

Were we to read only the announcements of entertainment, instruction and religious observances that took place in Morgins, we could easily forget that this was an internment camp, not an institute of lifelong learning. My first response now to the intense spiritual and intellectual ethos of Morgins, to the inspired use of 'free time', is astonishment and wonder: that during such devastation, internees could summon the moral and psychic courage to preserve Jewish life in its many and complex manifestations. Then my mind turns to the Warsaw Ghetto and Theresienstadt, where under conditions of unimaginable brutality, scholarly and cultural life continued until the end. Once again, I am caught in my familiar dilemma: how to honour the memory of the Jews doomed in concentration camps and ghettos without expunging from historical record the achievements, but also the misery, of refugee life in Switzerland?

Another scruple inhibits my unreserved proclamation of attainments in Morgins: will my testimonial to the spiritual resilience of the interned obscure the prevailing complexity of circumstances and perpetuate the egregious lie that the refugees were quite well off? Vacillation and ambivalence give way to trust in my readers, and I continue to cite from the pages of the Jewish weekly:

> 13 February 1944: The Jewish Cabaret Birmensdorf gave a guest performance: ten portraits, in which the old Jewish-chassidic life in the East unfolded before our eyes, scenes of joy and sorrow in the small Jewish towns.
>
> 18 February 1944: Rabbi Botchko, Rector of Yeshiva Eytz Chayim, spent this weekend in Morgins. He delivered several lectures there and at the *Oneg Shabbat* he specifically addressed the youth. Rabbi Botchko interpreted the words of the Torah in an easily understood, popular fashion in order to provide spiritual pleasure to all.
>
> 19 April 1944: Warsaw Ghetto remembrance.
>
> 5 May 1944: Piano recital by sixteen-year-old followed by a song recital.
>
> 26 May 1944: Free-time organizer complains about heavy workload and little appreciation. Lectures by well-known speakers are for the time suspended, but Beth Jacob courses and classes continue as does the youth outreach.
>
> 2 June 1944: Camp administrator describes Orthodox ritual of prayers with admiration ... All lectures deal with integrating Torah, secular studies, and vocational training for the post-war

> period.
>
> 14 July 1944: Max Fischer theatre and music: scenes from *Faust*: In camp such an undertaking is risky, but despite the primitive stage furnishings, it was a great success thanks to actors whose words and sensibility presented us with the ongoing struggles of humanity.
>
> 21 July 1944: Herzl-Bialik Evening: girls' choir; recital of poetry. Diploma for 14 who completed the Samaritan course. Chelm stories heightened the mood and relieved the monotony in Morgins.
>
> 18 August 1944: *Tisha B'Av*: silent sorrow like in a cemetery, honouring those who found no final resting-place.
>
> 6 October 1944: Days of Awe sermon: the good and bad suffered equally in the destruction of Jerusalem because of passivity; the good stood by and did nothing to prevent destruction, so too it is today.
>
> 12 December 1944: Talmud study groups led by camp residents. Theatre group, trio concert delighted music lovers. Lectures on life in children's homes.
>
> 29 December 1944: Hanukkah: Old and young gathered to attend the performance by children; it was a joy to see the youngest in costumes, reciting, singing, dancing; they gave their best Maccabbe songs and lit the Hanukkah candles. Gift packages to every child brought great pleasure. In the evening, the youth performed songs and recitations for the entire camp. It was a late night but light in all hearts.

We were a microcosm of scholars. A diverse population with its own talents and skills, we found sources of new knowledge in everything, everyone and everywhere. This mantle of learning was buttressed by the value placed on Jewish education; it was inconceivable that children would waste their days in random activity. Education, as distinct from schooling, was vast, open, ubiquitous; all yielded knowledge.

Our camp occasionally received visits from the outside world. From Geneva, the big city in our lives, a centre of pedagogic innovation (Piaget territory), came Madame Locafio. She was on a mission from a refugee relief agency. Well-assembled, middle-aged, crisply dressed, a neatly coifed grey head with an efficient bearing, she was a sharp contrast to our mothers and counsellors who long before had to abandon stylish fashion. She was Swiss, and we were children from all parts of Europe who shared a common flight from the Nazis and an unknown destiny. We were wild, undisciplined, undisturbed by parents who were careworn, often toopreoccupied with sorrows and concerns to pay full attention to us.

I don't know how I came to be in Madame Locafio's class. What I do remember is that along with lessons, she organized my three friends and me into a construction team to build a hut in the surrounding forest. I have a small sepia photograph taken on the day my friends and I completed our hut. Taken more than sixty years ago, it captured David, Gabor, Simon and me; we were about 7 years old. We stand very straight, gazing directly at the camera, purposeful expressions on our faces. We had, after all, accomplished a visible task, and we were the builders. Dressed in summer clothes, each of us holds a bundle of branches and ropes of lichen, the material demonstration of the day's effort and achievement. The sun breaks through the trees and we are illuminated like figures in a Renaissance painting. I have held onto this image so fiercely that were I to lose it, I think I would walk through the world dismembered. Why do I love this picture so? I want to inhale the scents of the fir forest in which we are pictured, my friends and I. We stand as firmly planted as the trees that surround us. The photograph celebrates a moment of tenderness and dignity; it is as though we stand for all children who have survived the war, in Switzerland.

I was a diligent pupil, encouraged by the aura of orderliness radiated by Madame Locafio. My one competitor vying for top standing was Hannah, who possessed a maturity and confidence beyond her years and certainly beyond mine. On the penultimate day of her stay with us, Madame gave us a spelling test. The highest score would receive a gold star, but, more importantly, she told us she had postage stamps from across the world, which she promised to distribute on the day of her departure. Stamps were our main currency in the camp. We had few books and fewer toys; friendships were bought and sold with the stamps we retrieved from wastebaskets and begged from adults.

I got a perfect score in spelling and won the gold star. Pleased as I was with the award, her stamps were the real prize: I couldn't wait to hold them, perhaps to trade them and win a friend in the deal. I can still feel the ground under my feet as I ambled down the hill to the bus stop where she would distribute these little trophies of the world. As I approached the bottom of the hill, I saw Madame Locafio leaning out of the bus window, waving goodbye to the assembly of children. I was too late. She had already given away the stamps and the fortunate philatelists, Hannah in the centre of the group, were peering at them, some still stuck to their envelopes, considering which worthless ones they would share with me. For the first time in my life I understood what it meant to feel betrayed by circumstances I brought on myself; I was the agent of my own disappointment.

After that incident in Morgins, postage stamps lost their lustre in my eyes. Now, decades later, they lure me back quite unexpectedly: my young granddaughter, Annika, is as besotted by philately as I was at her age. I now have a new partner and together we pore over every stamp, gasping at their beauty.

A good part of my life has been linked to schools and educational institutions. I perceive these many years as a continuum of elective affinities, and trace this predilection to the spirit infused into our childhood education, at a time and place where such endeavours were considered luxuries. Dazzling landscape, remaining for me the standard of natural beauty, enveloped us and seeped into our very being, imbuing our days and animating our education. The expanse of our surroundings, mountains, meadows and forests, became in time the reflector for our own expansiveness as young explorers of hidden and revealed worlds.

We lived in a realm endowed with significance: religious tradition, music and art. The joy of art, creating and living in beauty, I owe to Madame Greenbaum, one of our own, a refugee who may have been an artist/teacher before the war. A petite, delicate middle-aged woman, her presence opened my heart not only to the art we were to create, but also to an aesthetic that extended to the surrounding world. I absorbed from her a sensitivity to life itself. Held in the brightest room of the camp, her class was infused with the stillness of creation, the peacefulness of concentration. The hours we spent with her were an escape into a world wholly other than the chaos and storm that prevailed beyond the door of her art room. I attribute to her my introduction to the world of imagination, to create *ex nihilo* something of beauty and wonder: to bring nature onto paper by a drawing, to fabricate a miniature world by cutting and pasting.

One morning, standing at a work-table exuberant with colour and texture – paints, pencils, paper, raffia for the baskets we were decorating for Succot, the Jewish harvest holiday – I noticed a counsellor handing Madame Greenbaum a letter. She read it, frozen to the spot. And then she was on the veranda outside our classroom, bent over, holding a handkerchief to her eyes, quietly weeping. What had happened to our beloved teacher? Did the letter bring sad news? We all wondered. Later that day we heard that her brother had perished. She heightened all our senses and sympathies; before that incident I don't recall feeling another's grief as I did at that moment when I saw her back turned to us, her head lowered. Years later, a Kaethe Kollwitz drawing of a woman bent in sorrow immediately evoked her memory.

She planted the necessity of art in my life, and good fortune has placed me in its presence throughout my adult years. Living in New York during periods of vibrant artistic expression allowed me the joys of inhabiting the city's museums and galleries, of making art integral to my existence; merely stepping over the threshold to the Metropolitan Museum fills me with bliss. Always.

My move to Toronto, a city with modest claims to public art, left me bereft of those aesthetic pleasures that had sustained me in New York. Close to losing hope that my life would be replenished, I was hired to teach philosophy at Ontario College of Art. At the time, the college was undergoing a transformation; fundamental principles of art education were being challenged, and I passionately joined in the revolutionary ferment. Once again art permeated my life, but from another perspective: that of mentor, prod or gadfly, in a world of students, colleagues and artists who shared my passion. Madame Greenbaum's spirit guided me through those wondrous years.

I see myself in diverse settings in Morgins: some memories are generative, moving me into wider expanses and comprehension; others stand alone, unaccompanied, like the solitary outsider amidst a cohesive group. Still others resemble a still life, so contained that I wonder at their tenacity in my recollections.

Mornings are closest to the surface: I am sitting at a long table in our dining hall. The din overpowers the single voice, and I await the arrival of some tasty dish for breakfast, usually bread with margarine and jam and weak, milky coffee. I'm certain it was margarine and not butter that topped our bread, not because I knew the difference between the two but because my mother did. Her intolerance of ersatz extended to all matters and frequently got her into trouble. I remember one day of such disclosure: Mama had slipped out to a nearby farm in the village to buy some butter for me. She was discovered, still wearing her trench coat, a sure giveaway that she had strayed from the camp grounds. While I stood by her side, Mama received a stern reprimand from the camp head. She showed no sign of contrition, and I even detected a faint, mischievous smile on her face. To this day, I will not have anything but pure butter in the house, my lasting tribute to her daring.

Occasionally our breakfast would include a special treat of bread and minced onions. One of the servers, a cheerful, witty man, would twirl the tray over his bereted head and pretend to drop it as he delivered the glistening morsels to our table. He transformed mealtime into a circus of delight. Observing people closely, classifying their behaviour in my mind, I realized even then, I think, that any act, however routine or modest, could take on meaning if it was performed in the proper spirit. He was the jolly waiter, and all my future onion sandwiches were memorialized in his honour.

My father, who was a cook in the camp, also had a way of turning every meal into magic. He would make bread and butter into art by cutting it into little pieces like sculpture. I continue the practice for my grandchildren. I have a photo of him, standing with his kitchen buddies in front of the staff entrance to the hotel. I keep it in my kitchen, where I can look at it every day.

The bomb that fell on Morgins on 8 August 1944 was the only sign of war to shatter my sense of safety during the four years in neutral Switzerland. Out of nowhere it seemed to come, and then within minutes the entire camp population was in the open field adjoining the Grand Hotel. My parents and I huddled together; I felt warmed and secure. Some time passed. As there was no further indication of danger, my father stood up; he wanted to get a coat from his room. I clung to his leg and would not let him leave. He obeyed my cries and stayed with my mother and me. The story bruited about in the camp was of a German plane that had misfired, dropping the bomb, a small one apparently, on Morgins instead of on their target in France, just metres from the Swiss border.

Israelitisches Wochenblatt of that week treated the attack with greater seriousness: a youth hostel for Swiss apprentices had been hit and several occupants had been injured. The sponsors of the hostel, a Geneva-based organization, sent a letter of thanks to our camp head, noting the outstanding help given to the wounded by men and women from the refugee camp. I remembered the bomb incident vividly over the decades, but always as a casual mistake with few consequences. My only drama was fear that my father would leave and not return to us.

Childhood illness struck often, infecting all the young when it did.

During one measles epidemic, we lay in a darkened infirmary with little ministering; few Florence Nightingales hovered around us. One morning, a mother entered the infirmary and pulled the curtain, hoping, I imagine, to brighten our surroundings. This innocent act was to have lifelong consequences in the damage it caused. To protect my eyes from further injury at the time, a bandage covered them. Temporarily sightless, I recall being carried from place to place on my father's shoulders; to amuse myself I would try to guess where we were heading.

'We're passing the infirmary', I called out to Papa.

'How do you know that, Freydele?' he asked.

'We just said "hello" to the nurse, so we must be near the infirmary', I responded proudly, gesticulating with my hands. Papa praised me for my bit of inductive reasoning and although I could not see his expression, I could tell he was beaming. That sensation, riding high on top of his shoulders, seeing without eyes, has stayed with me; it was my introduction to the exhilaration of analytic thought.

Every new event in the camp captured our attention. We children were always ready to embrace whatever appeared in the way of novelty or excitement. As the end of the war came into view, intense effort went into establishing vocational training programmes. Motivated by concern for the refugees' post-war employability, these nationwide projects also served to hasten a much desired exit from Switzerland.

Morgins became a centre for corset making. Not surprisingly, the corsetiere and her trainees were women. Bolts of fleshy pink fabric lay on rows of long tables in the main hall of the Grand Hotel. A ballroom in better times, it now served as the commodious workshop for future corsetieres, where pieces of cotton cloth swirled as in a snowstorm. The children were given the task of picking the pins and needles from the floor. Magnets in hand, we crawled on all fours to grab hold of them. The instructor, a tall, bony, dark-haired woman in her late twenties, took her responsibility and her charges seriously, transforming the area into a hive of industry, women and children eager participants.

I spoke earlier of the contentment that I felt in Morgins, but only now do I think of happiness and joy. Based on the present, when pure joy is rare in my life, I wonder what it was I experienced. Amidst a world immersed in tragedy, albeit at a distance from me in Switzerland, what would I have felt? I look at photographs of that time and see a 6-, 7-, 8-year-old little girl, a *maydele*, as I would have been called in the Yiddish diminutive. Some of my gazes are serious, almost solemn, as in the photograph that celebrates our building a hut in the forest; in another I am on a swing on the front lawn of the Grand Hotel, behind me a white picket fence and the mountain. Festively dressed in a skirt, white sweater and vest, the universal ribbon in my hair, I have a knowing expression, a faint smile. A late spring setting, snow still on the ground, pictures a little pal and me, with my mother standing behind us, her arms around both of us. My mother and I are grim while the child next to me, her head bent towards me, is full of mischievous delight.

Another photograph, which came to me only a few years ago (saved for decades by my Aunt Rosa), is a group shot of thirty-one children and teachers/counsellors. In the centre of the front row, I literally stand out in this crowd of prankish, laughing children. This time I am dressed in overalls, still beribboned, hands in my hip pocket, and a satisfied, full-faced grin covers me. I was astounded to see my centrality in that group, placed in a position of leadership; in my small collection of childhood photographs, it is exceptional in the unalloyed joy it expresses. Was that a singular moment or a prefiguration?

I compare all these photographs, taken over two years and showing me in a variety of poses, contexts, moods and backgrounds, to the photos of refugee children I found in the Swiss archives and refugee memoirs: the range of expression is similar.

5

SEPARATIONS

Separation began by rationalizing the rupture of the primary family unit and then spread like a slow-burning fire, consuming vital traces of a former landscape. Once severance of fundamental bonds was sanctioned, it dilated almost seamlessly into a disengagement of other bonds: cultural, religious and linguistic. Displaced children became entities without psyches, floating through the world without spirit or core, whose lives could be managed pragmatically. Expedience and economic factors, as well as layers of anti-Semitism, some closer to the surface and others more hidden, all contributed to the end result of a subtle deracination.

Under the guise of universality and humanism, Swiss welfare organizations took children whose parents may have spent their youth in the shtetls (small towns of Eastern Europe) or in Jewish centres of urban Europe, and dropped them into the hamlets and mountain villages of Switzerland. Numerous Jewish children were thus cut off not only from their families but also from the connecting threads of their former lives – lives that had often just begun to exhibit self-consciousness. Such dislocation brought with it a loss of self and the loss of a centre. In its stead was offered an ersatz family, markedly different in character from their origins, from an expressive, emotional family ethos to a restrained, self-contained milieu. Not infrequently, a new religious faith was substituted, one with a history of hostility to Jews. Children who had witnessed and lived through unspeakable terror were now, in the safety of neutral Switzerland, exposed to yet another bewildering experience, for which they, their families and members of their people were expected to show gratitude.

Refugees are always at the mercy of the host country, the country that open-heartedly or grudgingly offers them a haven. The range of asylum seekers is almost as wide as humanity itself: the more privileged for whom dislocation is temporary; the impoverished for whom life has always been precarious; those for whom a catastrophic event destroys the delicate balance of daily life. And children, whose fates always depend on the adults of the world they inhabit. During the

Holocaust, Jewish children were the most vulnerable victims. As survivors, too, their susceptible condition held fast, whether in hiding or as refugees in neutral countries.

Writing about children who were refugees in Switzerland during the war, I am always quick to distinguish my own circumstances from those who were ill-fated. I crossed illegally into Switzerland with both my parents and brother, while other children came with only one parent (usually their mother) or without a parent, alone or in a group spirited across the border by rescue workers. I use 'ill-fated' to designate the absolute relativity of our predicament and the randomness of the brutality that prevailed. Because I can find no other words to signal both moral and circumstantial reality, it serves temporarily to designate the hierarchy of sorrow and loss.

My research into the separation of parents and children in Switzerland during the war has forced me to re-examine often overlooked or diminished aspects of my own experience. Because fate allowed me to stay in the same camp as my mother, I would compare my good fortune with that of the numerous children assigned to foster families; in that version I almost disappear as a victim of the war. I shift back and forth between what I've recollected and what I have uncovered in archives and personal interviews. My story continues to change and grow in complexity and elaboration.

What do I know of separation? When does separation first enter my life? The first moment I recall: I am nearly 5 years old. Mama and I are standing in the kitchen of our temporary apartment on Rue de Lausanne in Geneva. Our heads are tilted upward, like two children anticipating good news. A social worker from the Jewish Refugee Aid Committee has come to offer me a holiday in the mountains with a family who requested a Jewish refugee child for one month. Summer holidays, considered an essential ingredient for a happy Swiss childhood, were also extended to refugee children, whether or not they wanted such deliverance.

The mountains? They are high and remote, and perhaps I already know Mont Blanc, rising from Lake Geneva. To my eyes, lake, mountain and sky are one unbroken stretch of colour and texture. I picture myself moving heavenward, but the mystery of a heavenly journey is intertwined with my concern for Mama's earthly safety.

A month in the mountains, that first separation from my parents, has persistently wound its way back into my engagement with life and perception of reality. The tears of separating parents and children have remained an ever-present image of a sorrowful world. However, when

I first wrote about this event a few years ago, I tended to couch the story in detached, ironic language. A meagre reference to what must have been a traumatic episode was the only nod to my childhood. I titled that piece 'A Month in the Mountains'.

> The Summer of 1943 when I was five years old and living in Geneva, a young, enthusiastic social worker from a Jewish social service agency came to our apartment with an offer of a month in the mountains with a family who wanted a refugee child. This opportunity presented me with some concerns. Mountains and heaven held the same awe for me, and I wasn't sure I was ready for a journey to such heights. I worried as well about my mother who had a habit of dashing out into the street without regard to traffic; in my absence, who would insure her safe crossing? My anxiety about her began at a young age and would last throughout her life. The last time I saw my mother, two days before she died of a cerebral haemorrhage, she was running to catch the bus on Fort Washington Avenue in New York, confident that the oncoming cars would stop for her, and they did.
>
> An effusive young woman met me at the village train station and took me to the summer chalet she shared with her mother and sister. The first thing I saw as I crossed the threshold of their front room was a dog-skin rug, its black-and-white head and body splayed in front of the fireplace. I must have screamed in terror, because by the next morning it had disappeared and was never spoken of again. The day I left, I caught a glimpse of it behind the couch.
>
> I see that month in theatrical staging. In the first act, I, the young heroine, am introduced to a society altogether foreign, where I am taught manners and a new perspective on the world. I must have assumed my hosts were Jewish since I couldn't imagine my parents entrusting my care to anyone else. Their demeanour, however, was unlike that of any Jews I knew: they were relaxed, they laughed, and smiled easily, they were soft-spoken and genteel. Mother and her adult daughters attempted to bring me into the modern, secular world with its calm and cordial ways, as if the world were proceeding normally. They were Swiss, reflecting the peace that neutrality brings, mingling freely, if somewhat paternalistically, with the local rural population. They found pleasure in summer fairs.
>
> In the second act I rebel against their attempts to transform

> me. One incident highlights the tensions between my unshaped self and the new persona I was expected to take on: I am sitting on a log outside the chalet, sulking. Mademoiselle approaches and draws my attention to something, hoping, I suppose, to bring me out of my mopiness. I refuse her gesture, and when she says, 'Look at that!' I respond, 'I have eyes, I can see for myself.' She becomes angry and slaps me lightly on my bare leg; her message to me is clear: I have transgressed, I have been rude and unmannerly. Why does that scene on the log remain so vivid? Was it my way of rejecting her view of the world, even in such a literal and minor event? Was I telling her that I didn't want to be told what to look at, what to bring into my purview? The third act finds the heroine adjusting, if not enjoying her new life: she now laughs with her host family, she is charming, and her Pygmalions are pleased with their summer project.
>
> Later that same year, my mother and I are interned in the Morgins refugee camp. Mama is to undergo an operation for a goitre and insists on a Geneva hospital. Despite well-intentioned opposition from the camp director, Mama takes me with her to Geneva. A home has to be found for me while she is in the hospital, and this time I am consulted; to be accurate, my mother appeals to me in desperation. I agree to stay with the Orthodox Feuerwerker family, where I soon come to feel at home. During my stay with the Feuerwerker family, Mademoiselle from the mountains comes to visit, bearing puzzles and other educational toys. As we walk along the streets of Geneva, I mischievously tell her that I share a bed with Rachel, one of the family's adult daughters. Impassive, she stares straight ahead, yet I sense her disapproval of my sleeping arrangements; I enjoy her displeasure. I am once again in my milieu, returned to my people.

My apprehension about the month in the mountains was either dismissed or appeased. Did I protest at having to leave my parents? Was I afraid of suddenly being in a strange place with people I didn't know? Did my parents try to cajole me into this promise of a vacation, or was it assumed I would accept this gift with gratitude? Why were they so compliant, agreeing to a month away from them, as if we were living in the slums of Calcutta instead of wonderland Geneva? The root meaning of separation is 'without preparation'. With children in mind, the question is: are we ever prepared, can we ever really anticipate the parting, confident of a reunion with the beloved parent? At 5, was I not asked to have faith that I would be returned to my parents, that I would once again be admitted back to the safety of their embrace?

I recall many details of those years, yet I cannot find a trace of the emotions I must have felt. Looking back now as a mother and grandmother, whose children and grandchildren were gently and carefully prepared for a mere evening with a babysitter, I am filled with compassion for the child I was, a child expected to be grateful for what was given.

Separation and identity become intertwined at this point in the process of retrieval. Was I afraid then, in 1943, a 5-year-old, that I was lost to myself? That I had become another person? Why was I so eager to show myself, the real self I was, with the Feuerwerker family, and taunt Mademoiselle with my otherness? In reconstructing the past, reassembling fragments of childhood years, I came to anticipate certain breaks in my recollection, to recognize these interruptions. The vacant spaces were often bound to moments of departure from my parents, nor were my returns to them spared oblivion. So absolute was their disappearance that I was altogether unaware of these intervals in my life. It is too late to retrieve the missing pieces, to recover details of my history, now that my parents and brother are no longer alive. Remorseful beyond consolation for my failing, I turned to distant, inanimate sources.

My research journey to Switzerland in 2001 included a visit to the Geneva State Archives, which held the records of my family's border crossing and our activities in Geneva before assignment to internment camps. There, delivered by a young, taciturn archivist, I received my family's folder which contained confirmation of 'the month in the mountains'. A letter dated 28 June 1943, sent by the Geneva Section of Immigrant Aid to Children, addressed to First Lieutenant Poulin of the Bureau of Police, territorial district, Re: Johles, Frieda, number 2894, stated:

> Little Frieda Johles, born on 2/10/37 [wrong day of birth], Polish, who lives under military control with her mother in Geneva, at 53 Rue de Lausanne, was invited by Madame Hasenclever, 33c Avenue de Miremont, to spend one month's vacation with her in the mountains, in Diablerets, in the Canton of Vaud. Therefore, the little Johles girl is to leave on the first of July with Madame Hasenclever ... We would be grateful if you would permit the little girl to leave Geneva on that date for one month, to proceed to Diablerets and to issue her a travel and stay permit.

The file also contained a letter dated 30 June, addressed to Johles,

Frieda, daughter of Kasiel and Malka, *née* Jetti, Jewish, Polish national, at the present time under military control, last domiciled in Lyon. It set forth that she is freed from the military control of the police office of Geneva, and will proceed on that day to Diablerets, Canton of Vaud, to take up residence with Madame Hasenclever. 'Upon your arrival you will report in writing to the police of the district to whom you will be responsible from that day. The latter will determine the conditions of your stay. In the meantime, this letter serves as an identity paper.'

In the dimly lit hall of the archives, I laughed uncontrollably as I read the original 1943 letter requesting that the little Johles girl, 5 years old, under military control, report in writing to the police upon arrival at her/my destination. Following my initial response, I felt a certain delight: I did go to the mountains for a month, yes, my month in the mountains did happen. Why does it matter so much that records still exist to validate my memories? Was my recollection of that time not sufficient?

My thoughts moved between my account, written several years before the research trip, and the authentication of that same episode now before me. I was thrilled at the confirmation of my childhood intuition about my hosts' religion; judging by their name on the 1943 document, they were not Jews, and they probably did consider it their duty to civilize me. In the Geneva archives I also found scores of memos and letters about other refugee children's vacations: some joyous, others miserable. Regardless of the children's experiences, the correspondence on this subject occupied much time and filled many folders.

Although I escaped the worst forms of separation from my parents, I was not altogether free; over a lifetime I have preserved the bitter taste of those absences. Shortly after we arrived in Morgins, I recall Mama standing by my bed, about to kiss me goodnight and leave. The camp structure resembled a kibbutz: children slept, had their meals and were schooled in a separate building from their parents, whom they saw for some part of every day and for longer periods at weekends. In my memory, late summer dusk enters the dormitory window; light and life are outside, and I am to be abandoned inside. I cling to my mother and won't let her go. I scream, I bawl, I refuse reassurances that she'll be back the next morning. As always, she cannot bear my tears, and now she too is in a frenzy, her entire body a vessel of desperation. Her hands and arms now plead: 'What do you want from me?' Her entreaty, this last gasp of exasperation, touches me and calms me. I demand that she leave her sweater with me, as a promise that she will return to claim it the next day.

Another scene of separation, one which I have for years viewed as if I were behind the distanced lens of a camera: I watch the child I was, standing at the window of the centre hallway on the second-floor children's dormitory. I see my mother walking on the road by herself. She passes my house without stopping or looking up. Her head is slightly bent, characteristic of her departures from the here and now. I am alone; there are no voices and no sounds in this usually noisy place. Why is Mama not stopping; why is she alone and not with me when I am so close? The window is shut, I can't call out to her, and soon she disappears from my sight. Was this a recurring dream, which I've transposed to lived experience? Does it matter?

A night in New York, sixty years later: I lie awake. The anguish of separation has returned full force. I have been asked to take Mika, my 3-year-old granddaughter, to her nursery school because both parents have early morning appointments. At the request I turn rigid with foreboding. My daughter describes the school as a warm, nurturing place which Mika approaches with delight each day, and she reassures me that the parting moments are usually calm and loving: following a participatory activity, parents leave with a kiss, a hug and assurance of a reunion later in the day. All that night I imagine the heartbreaking scene, the moment I have to say goodbye to my granddaughter: she will wail, just as I did many years earlier and, like my mother, I will be helpless, unable to comfort her.

The next morning we set out, the two of us. I allow no hint of my fears to interrupt our lively conversation as we walk to Mika's school. Once there, in the cheery, spirited classroom, I panic; any minute now I will be caught in a grievous scene from which I will be unable to extricate myself. Mika exhibits no sign of distress; teachers welcome her affectionately and she chooses her first activity, a puzzle. I join her in assembling the pieces, and playfulness enters my being. This is not Morgins and she is not that little girl holding onto her mother's sweater. After completing our second venture, an intricate block structure, kisses and hugs are exchanged and I take leave of my happily engrossed granddaughter. Only outside the building do I take a real breath.

Throughout the war years and into the post-war period, the welfare of refugee children posed vexing questions: most urgent and contentious was the separation of mothers and children. The midpoint of my research in 2001 took place at the Swiss Federal Archives in Bern, which hold the files of the Schweizer Hilfswerk für Emigrantenkinder, SHEK, the major Swiss relief organization for refugee children. Established in 1933, SHEK facilitated the evacuation of children from war zones and provided for every detail of their welfare. In January

1942, with the influx of thousands of refugees from occupied Europe, the federal government turned over the responsibility for refugee children to SHEK, a trust to be shared with the Swiss Red Cross Children's Aid whose reputation during the Second World War was severely tainted. In collaboration with the Federal Council, it refused a haven to hundreds of Jewish children fearing this might compromise its status as a neutral, unbiased body. With the appointment of the Red Cross as partner came the designation of 'war damaged children' and, because of that specification, additional funds became available for relief work.

That assignment set the course for grievous consequences. SHEK was a non-sectarian organization, but during the years 1942 to 1945, 90 per cent of refugee children under its aegis were of Jewish background. Although Jewish children were the largest constituency in that welfare category, the influence of Jewish organizations in the settlement of children was minimal, indeed pitiful. Jewish welfare organizations were not empowered as caregivers, but they were the major financial supporters, with the largest portion of their budget coming from the Joint Distribution Committee in the United States.

The week before arriving in Bern, I had examined holdings in the Zurich Archives for Contemporary History where most of the Jewish refugee records are kept. These contain personal, social, cultural and religious documents of refugee life as well as the papers of Jewish organizational activity during the war. In that comfortable, brightly lit and brilliantly curated setting, I felt at home, surrounded as it were, by my people; this was the Jewish version of events.

Contrastingly, in the Swiss Federal Archives I was once again a foreigner as I sat at the long library table surrounded by the remainders and reminders of official wartime Switzerland. The voluminous SHEK files are contained in meticulously marked blue cardboard storage boxes, allowing for a systematic perusal. My first impression of the agendas and minutes of their frequent and regular meetings was that SHEK addressed the placement of Jewish refugee children with the same equanimity and efficiency they brought to every aspect of child welfare, such as clothing, nutrition and summer vacations. Their pragmatic tone and language lulled me at first into accepting the necessity of decisions made and procedures followed.

Predominantly women, these dedicated welfare workers and committee members, led by the revered Nettie Sutro, maintained with few exceptions that family placements were in the best interest of children: private homes would provide comfortable shelter, proper nutrition and reliable schooling. The primary concern of SHEK was to 'liberate' – to use Sutro's word – children from the deplorable conditions in the reception camps, where families were first quartered upon arrival. The camps, frequently in army barracks, were physically primitive: straw mattresses on cold floors and food unsuitable for children even during war rationing. Military discipline often complemented the oppressive warlike conditions: early morning roll-call, severe punishment for minor infractions, and the not infrequent presence of anti-Semitic staff who had little understanding of the refugees' predicament. Moreover, if mothers were to work, their children would be separated from them.

One of the earliest SHEK meetings to deal with this pressing problem was held on Saturday (the Jewish Sabbath) 31 October 1942 in Zurich. The following is a verbatim translation of the minutes:

> Sutro poses the question, at what age should the children be separated from the newly arrived mothers?
>
> Dreyfus thinks that the little children should stay in a kind of nursery while their mothers are interned in a nearby camp.
>
> Sutro is of the opinion that one can separate a child of four from mother.
>
> Seeburger finds that even a two-year-old child would not suffer the separation from the mother.
>
> Hohermuth asks, if it were not possible to establish a special reception camp for mothers and babies.
>
> Gerhard believes that children should not be placed together with their mothers in work camps.
>
> Sutro states that as long as the military reception camps remain, mothers and children should be separated, but not too far from one another. If, later on, free places in private families are found for the children, then parents should not be allowed to visit their children too often. She wants to free the children from the (reception) camps as soon as possible and to temporarily intern them in already established children's reception camps or with private families

On 30 October 1942, one day before that SHEK meeting took place, a member of a local chapter of the Jewish refugee relief organization reported on her visit to a camp near Montreux, where 300 women and 130 children were interned. She wrote that word had come from various sources of the intended evacuation of the children from the camp, separating them from their mothers and placing them in private families or children's homes; mothers were to be enlisted for the workforce:

> However beneficial this move may be for the children's physical state, this solution would be unspeakably difficult for the mothers. These women who have no home, no possessions, no future in sight, will be robbed of the only beam of light in their sad existence. If mothers and children living together proves an organizational difficulty, then the easiest solution would be to establish children's homes close by, so that the connection between mother and child can be maintained ... The separation of mother and child is injurious, an affliction to her spirit and morale that certainly cannot be justified. To some degree hardships of refugee life cannot be avoided, but the right of the mother must not be called into question. This is a universal, human matter, and independent of any religious issue.

Israelitisches Wochenblatt regularly reflected this concern about family separations. The leading article on 27 November 1942 was an open letter, identified only as coming from a highly-placed church source. The unnamed Christian author noted that refugee aid organizations, particularly Swiss women's groups and the Red Cross Children's Aid, were planning to separate children from their mothers, placing them in children's camps or with private families. Granting, that as presently managed, conditions in most reception camps were especially deplorable for children, it was nonetheless apparent that the emotional needs of refugee mothers were not being considered: 'Nothing is left to them but their children: separated from their deported relatives, from friends, from their homes, their possessions and freedom; and at present, some are far from their husbands. We must not take from them this last and most treasured thing.'

Continuing, the writer indicated that the separation might last years:

> Do we have the right to rob a mother who has already endured such hardships of her natural obligations and duties, leaving her to the emptiness and callousness of the camps ...? Let it not be said it is necessary for technical reasons. Love must be stronger than technical difficulties, and if love is genuine there is always a way to be found ... The greatest care must be given to act in the best interest of the child. A real mother cannot be replaced by a children's home nor can childhood years away from mother ever be recaptured.

The author referred to one transit camp where a Montessori teacher directed the kindergarten, and refugee women staffed the children's kitchen, thereby benefiting both mothers and children. Elementary classes could also be arranged if children were denied entry to local public schools and could be staffed by teachers from the community of refugees who longed to engage in their profession. 'Wrenching children from their mothers seems an inhumanity undertaken in the name of humanity ... Enough has already been torn asunder. That which still holds must be sacred to us.'

The same letter urged that visits and vacations with parents be assured for older children assigned to families near their high school or vocational training. Another plea addressed the needs of orphans, who in the absence of parents had formed attachments to other refugee families in flight; severing those bonds would be an injustice. The letter concluded with a plea to the community at large that 'mother's heart wins out'.

As it became evident that SHEK could not be stirred from its position of advocating private family placements, appeals for Jewish foster homes went out to all Jewish organizations and newspapers. The announcement in the 2 December 1942 issue of *Israelitisches Wochenblatt* began:

> The Swiss Relief for Immigrant Children has been entrusted with the placement and care of all children who, since this summer, entered Switzerland illegally. It is the wish of the authorities, and with the cooperation of the Swiss Red Cross Children's Aid, that all children between the ages of four and sixteen be brought to private families where they will forget the dark events of these last months and weeks, and once again become happy children. Younger children, under the age indicated, should whenever possible, and at the mothers' request, be left with them or in a collective setting near by.

The communication concluded with an exhortation by SHEK, and shared by all Jewish organizations, that as many Jewish children as possible be placed in Jewish homes, and although SHEK was already processing applications from diverse groups, it would gladly place each of its foster children in the most suitable milieu.

The editorial in the same issue responded to this order:

> According to this announcement by the Children's Aid, separating children from their mothers is a closed subject, a fact which is so disturbing to many Christian and Jewish groups. From our viewpoint, the unfolding efforts regarding this question should be resolved with consideration for the mother.

> Should the authorities, however, absolutely refuse such a solution, namely, that children stay with their mothers, then naturally it is to be most wished for that all Jewish children come into Jewish families.

To that end, willing Jewish families were asked to answer the call by return mail.

No longer able to effect a humane resolution to accommodate mothers and children in suitably arranged camps, the Jewish community was now left with compliance as its sole option, an option that it was able to realize with only modest success. 'Nine hundred Jewish children seek a Jewish home', read the headline in the 18 December 1942 issue of *Israelitisches Wochenblatt*. Invoking biblical and patriotic images, the article exhorted Jewish women to heed the cry of Mother Rachel weeping for her children. It stated that 1,000 Jewish children had been rescued by Switzerland and 100 had already found Jewish homes:

> Can motherly Switzerland now count on Jewish women taking the rest into their homes ... Who would hold back when it concerns helpless Jewish children? All Jews, after all, are responsible for one another ... The Jewish family who takes in a Jewish child performs the noblest *corriger la fortune*. Fate had intended that one thousand Jewish children perish; the Jewish family is redressing this misfortune ... Only those mothers who take in a Jewish child can look Mother Helvetia in the eye. Jewish children who now find a Jewish home guarantee the future of the Jewish soul ... A Jewish foster child with all his individual potential is a far greater teacher to every Jewish mother than she herself is to her own children. For the child is reminder, warning and hope in one person ... There is only one response to the injustice committed against the Jews: rebuilding the next generation; anything else will, in the end, appear as sanctioning this injustice ... Isaiah said the widow must receive justice and the orphan his bread. The entire Jewish people is now both widowed and orphaned. So, give them their justice and their bread and the nine hundred children their Jewish home.

Once the EJPD assigned the welfare of refugee children to SHEK and the Swiss Red Cross, Jewish voices were effectively silenced in deciding the placement of Jewish children and the frequency of parental visits, which were at first allowed four times a year and later increased to once every six weeks. The SHEK documents describe the emotional scenes attending the return of children to their foster families after one of their infrequent parental visits; their solution to the heartbreaking leave-taking was to establish neutral islands, 'vacation centres', for family weekends.

The lack of Jewish political influence and power was felt most sharply and painfully in the assignment of Jewish children to Christian families. Approximately 22,000 Jewish refugees outnumbered the original Swiss Jewish community of 18,000 in a country of over four million. It made numerical sense that a greater number of Christian families were available as foster parents; however, it was also true that Jewish families were more generous in supporting refugee children financially than they were in opening their homes to them. Appeals for Jewish foster families, initiated in 1942 and continuing through the war years, were not sufficiently heeded, and as a result, most of these Jewish children found themselves in Christian foster homes.

In its defence, the small, overtaxed Jewish community was beset by an avalanche of needs that it felt morally obligated to meet. Foremost was the rescue of Jews fleeing the 'Final Solution'; border crossings were life-and-death points, but even in the interior of Switzerland there were tragic incidents of deportations to the occupied side, leading to almost certain death. Maintaining and supporting religious and cultural life were also constant concerns of the Jewish community: arranging education for children and youth, dietary requirements for the Orthodox, and holiday provisions for all the refugees.

The Jewish community's role in protecting the religious life of children was now relegated to the Division for Religious Care of Children (RBK), an administrative department of the Swiss Jewish Association for Refugee Relief (VSJF). Established in 1942, the mandate of RBK was the arrangement of religious instruction for children aged 7 to16, through the services of itinerant teachers or through designated religious schools under its aegis. The provision of textbooks, phylacteries, matzos and other ritual requirements was a constant concern for the department. Outlining the various duties and responsibilities of the agency and their designates, an early RBK document stated unambiguously that the placement of children was not within its domain but belonged exclusively to SHEK and the Swiss Red Cross Children's Aid to whom the secretariat would forward all necessary reports.

Because SHEK's placement policy did not assume a Jewish environment as an unconditional principle or as a legitimate right, Jewish children in Christian homes were cast into multiple levels of displacement. Deprived of parental proximity and affection, they were also alienated from their religious traditions and practices. This disregard for children's psychological and spiritual needs robbed them of their role in safeguarding Jewish continuity, a charge that certainly the more mature among them had assumed was theirs. And yet there were exceptions: in one canton SHEK sent a very moving letter to a local school district regarding Sabbath observance for Orthodox boys.

Barely veiled contempt seeped through the correspondence between SHEK and Jewish women's relief organizations as the latter tried to wrest what had now become privileges for Jewish refugees. In one particularly vitriolic letter on the subject of High Holy Days invitations from Jewish families, Nettie Sutro argued that not all the children who were now orphaned came from religiously observant homes, and to expect them to be brought into an orthodox environment seemed not to respect the spirit of their departed parents. Moreover, she added, 'If Jewish women really want to help the deported mothers, they ought to take more children into their homes, and not only over the holidays but for the next six months. And to women, who in all kindness have already taken children into their homes: keep them, and do not return them to us when their limited time is up.'

The editorial in *Israelitisches Wochenblatt* on 17 September 1943 took a stand on the issue of denying a Jewish environment during the High Holidays to children raised in non-observant homes: 'Proclaiming a "tradition of non-tradition" is very spurious. One can imagine if Christian children were denied a Christian environment during Christmas time because their parents were irreligious! What a storm would erupt in Christian circles over such an idea! Moreover, the High Holy Days are celebrated in all Jewish homes, not only among the "Orthodox".'

Foster parents were instructed by SHEK to respect the religious traditions of Jewish children: they were not to take them to church services or Sunday School; they were to accommodate the children attending religious school or classes with itinerant teachers appointed by the Jewish community. Unhappily, these regulations were not always followed. As concern grew for the religious fate of Jewish children, rabbis and other entrusted members of the Jewish community investigated and reported on conditions in Christian foster homes.

Lists of what came to be known as 'Endangered Cases' were sent to SHEK by the RBK with requests for placement changes. These were some of the children at risk:

> J.L., born in 1934: he attends Christian Sunday school.
> V.R., born in 1938: foster parents refuse religious instruction and expose him to missionary influence.

C.F., born in 1935: she is being raised as a Protestant and is greatly at risk.
C.E., born in 1932: foster parents refuse religious instruction, claiming that his parents do not want him to receive instruction. Rabbi Dr G. says that parents do want instruction for their child.
A.S., born in 1935: her mother pressures for transfer to a Jewish milieu. The child was secretly baptized, and the foster parents take her to church. Her mother wants Jewish instruction for the child. The case was reported on 9.4.45 to the Argau division.
D.T., born in 1937: her environment in a convent endangers her.
A.G., born in 1937: foster parent is minister and she is undeniably at risk.
H.G., born in 1930: he has to work long hours in the foster family's bakery and seems to have no time for religious instruction. Request to investigate whether the child is at risk; if not, he should receive instruction where he is (in Habkern).

All but one of these cases were in rural areas, removed from urban Jewish communities, Jewish influences and education. Jews have generally fared better in cosmopolitan settings and this instance of misery was no exception. The provincialism inherent in most rural areas did not bode well for encouraging children's attachment to Judaism nor for sustaining Jewish continuity.

Children of my age comprise the list of 'Endangered Cases'. I recall my immersion in an unmediated Jewish world where Yiddish, *mame loshen* (mother tongue), surrounded me, its comforting sounds and soothing words enveloping my being; where holidays were celebrated in song and performance; and where art framed our days. I flinch at the thought that I too might have been among those ill-starred children whose lives were spiritually and emotionally diminished, perhaps permanently. For me, Jewishness meant an intimacy with God who watched over me and who was ever present.

Reflecting on the Jewishness pervading my years in Switzerland during the war, I recognize *yiddishkeyt* as a second home with its attendant familiarity, contentment and security. The authorities viewed it as a dispensable detail during severe times, and they gave little weight to the importance of Jewish influence precisely during times of dislocation and uprootedness. Children live not only within a family; they also inhabit a cultural, linguistic home, and this expression of their being was unattended by placement in Christian homes. My own brief exposure to a Gentile family for a mere month in the summer, followed that same year by a stay with an Orthodox family, underlines the disparity between the two, and has been imprinted in my memory for a lifetime. The family that hosted me that summer was kind, thoughtful and diligent in caring for me, but we belonged to different worlds, and at that time in my young life I was not prepared for the universality of humanity. I wanted my own, familiar, customary ways. The orthodox Feuerwerker family, while not replacing my parents, shared the same world, one that I recognized and understood; more importantly, I could be myself and did not have to adjust to an entirely foreign way of being in the world.

Hundreds of children who arrived in Switzerland without their parents, some already orphaned by the war, were separated from their siblings and other Jewish children and placed in foster homes. Were SHEK and the Red Cross not committed to the primacy of a family setting, more Jewish children's camps could have been established where counsellors and teachers from their own background would have provided understanding and continuity with their past. But ideology was not the only consideration in the choice of placements. Economic factors entered the picture as well; it was less costly to place children in private homes, even with subsidies to the foster parents, than to support communal settings, and this money-saving opportunity was not lost on the Swiss Children's Relief organizations.

The list generated by the RBK represented only an abstract of the passionate struggle for the souls of Jewish children during those bitter years. The correspondence between the RBK and the various SHEK chapters exposed the uneasy, strained relations between these two child welfare organizations, reflecting disparate sensibilities and powers. Underlying much of what passed in their letters was the unequal status of the two: SHEK and the Swiss Red Cross had the imprimatur of the state while the Jewish organizations were allowed only a designated and limited voice. These were two benevolent groups, one flaunting its non-sectarian stance under the benign cover of universality, the other beleaguered and besieged by the very reason of its specificity.

Cognizant of the annihilation of their co-religionists in the rest of Europe, the Jews of Switzerland were demeaned in their attempts to safeguard the spirit of the small remnant who had escaped. Conspicuously Jewish, the Orthodox were singled out and marginalized, frequently censured for their 'narrow-mindedness' and ingratitude. Gratefulness was expected for the dedicated work of SHEK as well as for the generosity of Swiss Christian families; accordingly, the leading Jewish groups did not fail to pay tribute to their benefactors.

Complaints by Jewish agencies that Christian foster parents were violating the religious rights of Jewish children were often met with hostility and denials. Dismissing the problem of 'endangered children' (quotes in the original), a member of the St Galen chapter of SHEK asserted that only minimal transgressions in this sphere had come to their attention. Moreover, she claimed, there were children from non-observant homes who did not wish to attend religious classes, and 'We have no grounds nor justification to support the missionary zeal of the Swiss Jewish Association for Refugee Relief (VSJF). We are a non-sectarian relief organization and we tolerate no "mission" [quotes in original], neither Christian nor Jewish. Granting asylum to these children and saving their lives allows no religious community to claim possession of these children under our authority.'

Referring to parents' wishes, her letter continues: 'We know from our own experience that this so-called "expressed" [quotes in original] wish of the parents is often a result of Jewish pressure and we therefore check every case; where we are convinced of the honest wish of the parents, we naturally consider taking that into account.'

This sanctimonious defence of children's religious rights came from the organization that promoted and implemented the separation of 4-year-old children from their mothers who were under pressures we can only imagine.

That same week in April 1945, another chapter of SHEK responded to the controversy surrounding children in Gentile foster families. Issued by the Geneva office, the letter, addressed to the central office in Zurich, rose to heights of scorn rarely seen in their formal correspondence. On the subject of children attending church or Sunday school, the writer drew upon her own experience of growing up in a village where her Protestant family was in the minority. As a result, she and her siblings attended Catholic services weekly and knew the rosary as thoroughly as their Catholic neighbours. Despite that, she concluded in her homily, no one in her family considered conversion to Catholicism. The moral of her tale ensued:

> It does not follow to say that Jewish children are religiously endangered if they attend church or Sunday school. If the Jewish religious community is really convinced of that, then they must place Jewish children in a glass house where they are hermetically insulated from every Christian influence. I strongly doubt that more than a minority of the Jewish children we now have in Switzerland were raised in observant Jewish homes. Preventing

> children taken in by a Christian family from going to church with them, or from attending Sunday school, represents an emotional burden far greater and certainly more damaging to children than what they hear in church or Sunday school. Basically, they hear nothing bad there ... We must think about living with and not in opposition to one another. That certain foster families lack the necessary tact and respect for Jewish beliefs is certainly possible, and very regrettable. But that is no reason to say that children are at risk who attend Evangelical services or Sunday school.

This explicit letter, like others from SHEK, minimized and trivialized the incidence of non-compliance by foster parents: 'A few cases have come to our attention but if the child is unwilling to attend (Jewish) religious instruction, in my opinion, coercion makes little sense and encourages only opposition.'

Revealing ignorance and disdain for the predicament of the Jewish community, she concluded:

> General observations: I find this entire method of questioning not only unpleasant but very regrettable. One must really ask oneself why and for what reason the Christian families in such numbers, as was the case, took in Jewish children. Even if a small percentage (of the 5,000 Jewish children, four were baptized, I heard) actually were to have left the Jewish faith, that is no ground to think of the rest of the children as religiously at risk. I believe that an essential task of our entire work with children exists to promote and encourage consideration for others' beliefs and not to build barricades between particular persuasions. The position taken by the VSJF achieves the opposite and is certain to be misunderstood by the Swiss people. According to the attitude of the VSJF all Jewish children should be removed from Christian families, since everywhere a child is at risk going to Christian services or Sunday school. That would be horrible, both from the view of the child and the general public.
>
> With friendly regards, B. Hohermuth.

In the Federal Archives, so many years later, I read the letters and the minutes of meetings. I imagine myself at the assemblies of these well-intentioned people, all concerned with the present and future of

Jewish refugee children: children who have crossed the border with parents or in groups with guides; others who have crawled to safety through barbed wire, unaccompanied by adults. As I enter more deeply into that past, I become the mother faced with impossible choices, and I am less persuaded by the view that we cannot judge history from our present perspective. I revise my judgement and view the predicament of those mothers as unnecessarily cruel, pressed to part from their children, to surrender them to foster families. What mother would not be lured by the chance of a 'normal life' for her children with its promise of physical comfort and a good education? Mothers were also terrified by the possibility of expulsion should they refuse the authorities' orders. Traumatized by the horrors they had witnessed before their escape and the many known incidents of *refoulement*, their fears were not unfounded.

While in that projected role, I come across a short article in a crumbling newspaper reporting on the disasters in occupied France in 1942. As rumours spread that orphaned children would be spared deportation to concentration camps, a number of Jewish mothers committed suicide hoping to save their children. We now know that, tragically, these mothers' deaths did not prevent the liquidation of orphanages in France.

Later, at home, reunited with my grandchildren, I continued to review the material from Swiss archives. The presence of then 5-year-old Annika and 7-year-old Yaneev cast me into another role: I began to think like the child taken from her mother. In becoming that child, I recognized that my feelings had been rarely discussed, that my life had been decided and managed as a physical being without regard to emotional and spiritual needs. While it is true that much of the psychological research on separation anxiety came to the fore only after the Second World War, there were certain perceptive and sympathetic voices during the war years. Every now and then an advocate on behalf of children was heard: a column in *Israelitisches Wochenblatt* of 21 July 1944, headed 'Children and Parents under Separate Roofs', called forth Switzerland's own Pestalozzi, the illustrious educator who promoted the family unit as the unequalled nurturer of children. In her brief piece, the author, 'Deborah', asks: 'What have the immigrant children done to deserve losing their best teachers? Who is in a sorrier state, the orphan or the child kept away from parents? What is darker: a natural cave or an elaborately constructed, endless tunnel?' The author continues, alluding to the brutality of infrequent parental visits: 'The children are allowed to see their parents only every three months to avoid the wrench of parting. But meanwhile how painful the separation? Hard arithmetic for the child's spirit.'

In my newly-found censorious stance, I wonder whether the show of concern for mothers, fleeting as it was, can be attributed to expediency: easier for welfare workers to see separation from the mother's standpoint than from the child's, easier to sway mothers, to allay their fears. Nettie Sutro counted among her achievements not only placing most children, but also calming mothers faced with the loss of their children, who understandably did not want to part from them.

In speaking to friends about the records of 1942, which I found in the organizational holdings of the Swiss archives, I describe the deliberations about the placement of children as 'cold-hearted'. My friends take exception to these harsh words, arguing that they are too strong, perhaps applied unfairly to well-intentioned acts of sixty years ago. I listen, but I am not convinced.

Examining the punctiliously kept records of SHEK, I vacillate between admiration and rage: admiration for their unstinting dedication to the fate of the 5,000 Jewish children whose care they assumed with fervent enterprise, and rage at the insensitivity of their discussion and implementation of separating parents and children. Separation: I hear the word and see only a violent tearing asunder, ripping the child from the mother, both left hysterical by the act. Separation: only death can match its pain. I have always empathized with parents and children who refused to be separated during the Holocaust, even when it meant certain death. Separation for the children is abandonment.

What was the sequence of events that determined the destiny of Jewish refugee children, and how did each step foreshadow the next? Tracing events from the standpoint of great temporal distance, it is almost impossible not to attribute a causal relation to acts which at the time may have appeared quite independent of each other. Without slipping into an infinite regress, some background is necessary to comprehend the complexities of this particular moment in Holocaust history. Jewish children were marked at the very start of the war in fundamentally different ways from other refugee children who spent the war years in the safety of Switzerland. Because they were Jews, the Nazis and their collaborators in every occupied European country hunted them. If they were caught in flight at the borders of Switzerland and turned back, they faced deportation to concentration or extermination camps and almost certain death.

Other neutral countries – Sweden, Spain, Portugal – did not separate families. At this point in reconstructing the narrative of Jewish refugee children, the conditional case is irresistible. Had the federal justice department not mandated that all able-bodied adults be segregated from those unfit for work – children, nursing mothers, the sick and elderly – and subsequently, had the authorities not assigned the placement of Jewish children to SHEK and the Swiss Red Cross; had these nonsectarian children's relief agencies been less zealous in implementing the separation of parents and children; had the Jewish community been given the right to determine the destiny of its refugee children; had all these decisions taken a different turn, then one may assume that family separation would have been unthinkable, irreconcilable with compassion for the refugees' devastating circumstances.

Had the will of the Jewish community prevailed in the placement of unaccompanied children, many of them already orphaned, it would have been unthinkable, indeed incompatible with Jewish values, to place them with Christian families. Establishing a greater number of communal Jewish homes for these children would have prevented what came to be called the 'endangered children' syndrome. Instead, what befell individual children was the theft of their birthright, and the community the loss of children to Christianity.

The decision on the part of SHEK and the Red Cross to assign children to foster families was based on a number of factors, each intensifying the others. The guiding principle informing the actions of SHEK and the Red Cross is open to grave questions. If indeed family life was the best arrangement for war-traumatized children, then surely supreme efforts ought to have gone into keeping them with their own parents. However deplorable conditions in some camps may have been, had the priorities been based on humane considerations, modifications to existing camps could have been made. Moreover, in 1942, the many hotels for which Switzerland was famous were empty and available for refugees; indeed, many did ultimately become sites for refugee camps.

I try to imagine my children and grandchildren, whose faces are now closer to me than my own from sixty years ago, as strangers in a strange land, robbed of continuity and identity; as foreigners in a xenophobic country; as children whose memories were mere fragments, fragile to the touch, forced to abandon those vestiges and assume a new persona with good cheer and gratefulness. Unhappily, Jewish refugee children were victims of an all too human trait: invoking universality, we deny specificity to others, while guarding our uniqueness; our own identity is never dispensable.

Once empathy and moral imagination took secondary place in the commitment to children, management came to be seen as care; responsibility passed for humanity and fellowship. It must be noted that Switzerland suffered only secondary inflictions during these years of upheaval and destruction in the rest of Europe. Therefore, much more could have been done to preserve Switzerland's claim as a humanitarian haven: borders could have been more generously opened and those let in could have been treated as fellow human beings.

Yet however bleak the picture that emerges, there were among the citizens of Switzerland those who cried out against such cruelty and devoted themselves to the welfare of refugees.

1. The author, age 6, Morgins refugee camp, c.1943.

2. The author, age 7, with her mother and a young friend in Morgins refugee camp, c.1944.

3. The author, age 7, and her friends after building a hut in Morgins refugee camp, c.1944.

4. Kitchen staff in Morgins refugee camp. The author's father, Kasiel Aba Johles, second row, fourth from the left, holding coffee pot, c.1944.

5. A postcard picture of Morgins.

6. Jewish children in Morgins refugee camp c. 1944. The author, age 7 is standing in the front row wearing overalls.

7. Author's drawing exhibited during the 'International Study Week on the War Damaged Child', July 1945.

8. Author's self-portrait exhibited during the 'International Study Week on the War Damaged Child', July 1945.

9. The author's mother, Malka Komornik Johles, in Switzerland, c.1945.

10. The author's father, Kasiel Aba Johles, in Switzerland, c.1945.

11. The author's brother, Max Johles, in Switzerland, c.1945.

. . . spaziert in Luzern

12. Cartoon in refugees' newspaper, 'Ueber die Grenzen', c.1945: 'A stroll in Lucerne.' Note on tree: 'The Lucerne promenade is forbidden to refugees'. Courtesy of Archiv Für Zeitgeschichte, Zürich, ETH.

13. Cartoon in refugees' newspaper, 'Ueber die Grenzen', c.1945: 'Switzerland: "I'm sooo happy and sooo proud to have you all with me".' Courtesy of Archiv Für Zeitgeschichte, Zürich, ETH.

14. Students at the ORT training programme, Geneva, 1946. The author's mother, Malka Johles is second from the left.

15. The author, age 8, with her cousin Fritzi Rosner (now Rosner Shay) in Zurich, summer 1946.

16. The author, age 9, and her parents as new immigrants in Boston, 1947.

17. The author and her cousins, Paula Brown (now Doress-Worters) and Emmanuel Brown, in Boston, 1947.

6

CLARENS: SHIFTING GROUND OCTOBER 1945–FEBRUARY 1946

1945

International Events
17–26 January: Thousands of Jews die on a 'death march' after the Auschwitz-Birkenau concentration camp is abandoned. By the end of the war, hundreds of thousands have died on marches as ghettos and concentration camps are evacuated.
27 January: Soviet troops liberate Auschwitz.
7–9 May: German capitulation; end of the war in Europe.
8 May: Soviet troops liberate Theresienstadt.
26 June: The United Nations Charter is signed.
22 December: The 'Truman Directive' allows displaced persons, especially children, entrance to the US.

Swiss Refugee Policy
8 February: 1,200 Jews from Theresienstadt reach Switzerland.
25 February–1 March: Swiss Refugee Conference in Montreux.
14 September: The EJPD relaxes restrictions on refugees' freedom of movement. (Information from the Bergier Report [Commission of Experts])

My reflections on Clarens were to be a detour in my memoir, a slighter chapter, given the brevity of my stay in the refugee camp, Beau Site. In my thoughts, Morgins had remained, while Clarens, where I stayed for an interval of only five months, was often an afterthought in awakened memories of my refugee years, barely worth recounting in normal times. I'd held onto certain images of those months with a vividness and tenacity that belied their short duration, but they were like photographs without the accompanying story. Recollections and linkages, parallels and metaphors receded when I touched the pen: I encountered a stony block, immovable when I attempted words. The internee was interning her thoughts: it was as though the very act of writing about Clarens drew me back to those years, and I assumed the persona foisted on me then: expected to be silent, undemanding, and above all, appreciative.

With great effort I pieced together my own life in the context of the historical events in the world around me. I looked back at myself during those months in Clarens, our second and last refugee camp, and saw an emerging being, moving – slowly at times – into a more diverse, encompassing world that beckoned but also repelled. Already a refugee for three years, I was then an 8-year-old girl, assuming a distinct persona, time and place collaborating to open new vistas. But just as the end of the war brought its own miseries to many, so my personality unfolded and expressed its own predicaments and dilemmas. With the war's end, turmoil and dislocation accompanied endeavours to restore a fragmented world. That time of worldwide convergence and contradiction coincided with my own groping for self-definition; conflict and opposition coexisted with transitions and thresholds in my personal evolvement.

In October 1945, my parents and I were assigned to Camp Beau Site in Clarens, a village imperceptibly linked to the city of Montreux. At that time, refugees were leaving Switzerland; some returned to their former homes in Belgium, Holland and France, while others left for Palestine, the Americas or Canada. Camps were consolidated and remaining internees transferred to other parts of the country

Still in a refugee camp, but with changes in structures and strictures, we were now situated within walking distance of Montreux, the 'Swiss Riviera', on Lake Leman (also known as Lake Geneva). Beau Site, like the Grand Hotel in Morgins, had been a resort before the war. The Swiss, with their world-renowned talents as hoteliers, once again provided the refugees with lodgings of splendour unknown to most before the war. The elegant, many-windowed dining hall was shared by all; families were seated at their own tables, like guests at a resort. My parents' spacious, comfortably furnished room, overlooking the surrounding plateaued countryside, included a divan and a bidet, which enchanted me. I cannot recall the children's quarters with any clarity, but we spent more unstructured time *en famille*. Proximity to the splendid city of Montreux brought back the months I had spent in Geneva prior to internment in Morgins.

We left the remote alpine village of Morgins, with its single road between mountains and the thick fir forests that had enclosed and bound us to a circumscribed Jewish life. As a younger child in Morgins, I was the beneficiary of a cohesive community, integrated at every level and sphere. The camp had been my home, my surrogate extended family. I'd been too young to fully realize that we were in a temporary haven:

like most children my age, I had lived in the present, giving little thought to yesterday or tomorrow. That unchanging world was interrupted by my brother's departure in 1945, on one of the first Youth Aliyah transports to Palestine. While in the youth home, Versoix, during most of the Swiss years, Max had been a presence in my life only intermittently, but now that he was on a kibbutz in Palestine, as settled as a 19-year-old could be, his absence felt deeper to me, more absolute. He would no longer appear unexpectedly as he had one day when I happened to glance out the window of my classroom and saw his blond, curly head approaching. Far away, across the world now, he was in a place of honour, where my parents and I might join him in the near future.

The easing of rules and restrictions in the camps, and in Switzerland as a whole, echoed in my being: in the open landscape of Clarens we were allowed greater freedom to roam than in the past; a new school seemed foreign and inhospitable, yet also novel and stimulating. I responded to the changes and embraced this wider universe which lured me – but I knew not where. My inner and outer landscapes complementing each other, my perspective on the world was expanding, broadening. When we left the camp for school each day, we were on our own in a world that did not know or cherish us. With freedom came the responsibility to shape a self, to act upon the world and to make judgements about appropriate behaviour.

In 1945, a confluence of events and circumstances (including the Allied victory and world opinion) effected more humane policies and behaviour toward the refugees. The Swiss government was now on the defensive, conscious of its image among the nations. As one public figure said, 'Former refugees may now be leaders of the reconstructed world and they may not have such warm feelings towards Switzerland.'

Survivors of Theresienstadt, Buchenwald and Bergen-Belsen were, at this time, admitted to Switzerland as refugees. The Buchenwald boys, as they were called, liberated by the British, were lured to Switzerland by the United Nations Refugee Relief Association with the promise of vocational training. Initially, these young, traumatized victims were treated like criminals, kept behind barbed wire; only after public and media outcry against such cruelty were more compassionate measures introduced.

The Montreux Conference on Refugee Rights, held in February 1945, to deal with problems and issues of repatriation and transmigration of refugees, was attended by government officials, welfare workers and refugees. This was the first time democratically elected refugees were included in discussions touching on their welfare. The conference proposed immediate reforms in camp regulations: greater freedom of movement, lifting of restrictions, expanded autonomy in camp organization and greater focus on retraining. Refugees were no longer to be restricted like prisoners of war, and families were to be reunited. Psychological harm suffered by refugees was at last acknowledged and highlighted in various reports. The study week on 'the war-damaged child', held in Zurich in September, brought together mental health workers from across Europe. Refugee children were now accepted by local public schools.

In 1945 Swiss Asylum came to an end. Despite everything that had now been revealed about the fate of Europe's Jews during the Holocaust and its aftermath, the Swiss government held fast to its fear of foreign influence, *Überfremdung*. Even when their numbers accounted for less than 1 per cent of the population, Jewish refugees were expected to leave the country as soon as possible, either through repatriation to Western Europe or through transmigration to a third country. (Rothmund, the architect of Swiss refugee policy, had gone on to greater heights, representing Switzerland at the Intergovernmental Committee on Refugees.)

While most other (non-Jewish) refugees and displaced persons in Europe could re-establish lives in their former homes, Jews found many countries closed to them. Germany and Austria, as sites for reconstruction, were out of the question for most: too much blood on their earth. Swiss officialdom as well as benevolent welfare workers pressured stateless Jews who repudiated German and Austrian repatriation to resettle in those countries. America and Britain also endorsed the return to Austria and Germany since it would ease their own displaced persons problems. Jewish organizations as well as the Montreux conference discredited that option and urged the severing of all ties with Germany. Poland, for hundreds of years the home of many Jewish people, offered no welcome to the minute remnant who had survived the extermination camps; pogroms were once again fomented and thousands were massacred. The United States quota was meagre, and for natives of Eastern Europe almost non-existent. Immigration to Palestine was severely restricted by the British; the certificates issued were assigned to urgent groups, such as orphaned children and youthful survivors of concentration camps. These heartless policies created once again the plight of the wandering Jew.

To expedite the refugees' speedy departure, vocational training courses were established throughout Switzerland. Where once retraining was a rarity and limited to domestic work for women, programmes were now ubiquitous: persons with trades would be deemed more employable in receiving countries.

The number of camp children had shrunk by 1945, and schooling for us had become something of a lottery. We were parcelled out to different schools in the area, and three girls from the Beau Site camp attended the local public school. Entering a new school, l'École Chantilly, which was radically different from the one in Morgins, I was expected to make a go of it, to fit in and confront a new curriculum. In that setting we were a tiny minority in a class of Swiss children who might never before have seen a Jew.

In the move to l'École Chantilly, I was doubly dispossessed: I lost the content and ambiance of a Jewish education and, closer to my heart, I lost the coterie of camp boys in whose midst I had always felt my true self. Gender-segregated classes deprived me of the comfort, amusement and adventure the boys personified and bestowed in countless, diverse ways. I had basked in their unstinting acceptance and loyal friendship, and delighted in their plucky stand toward the adults, which spurred my own rebellious spirit. I missed their presence, their antics; there was no one now with whom I could conspire against authority. Above all, they were spirited and funny, great companions. The boys were without pretensions; their indifference to appearance served me well. With a mother who shared their nonchalance in this area, I was freed from embarrassment about style of dress that I felt among the fastidious girls. I was now in foreign territory, in girl country, and in a Gentile land that rejected my essential nature.

Our teacher was a dour, middle-aged woman with a large, dimly-lit face, who seemed barely able to endure our presence. I do not recall one kind word or smile from her; when she addressed us, it was always as 'the new girls,' and our nameless state lasted to our final day in her class. Returning the favour, I have banished her name from my memory. The pupils were more approachable, but we remained strangers, outsiders, with few demonstrations of affection, interest or even curiosity; no invitation was ever extended to visit their homes.

Classes in Morgins had been conducted in an intimate, homey fashion befitting our former family camp. There, a disputatious ambiance was the norm and our argumentative spirit was appreciated, considered as an auspicious beginning to a future as Jewish scholars. Now, formality and arbitrariness prevailed; rules could not be ignored nor their merits debated with the teacher. Shortly after my arrival, the new regimen had visible and unforgettable consequences. Instructed to ask permission to leave for the bathroom, we were, however, not guaranteed an exit. One afternoon, close to the end of the school day, I raised my hand, but the teacher paid no attention. Despite every attempt at bladder control, I peed on the floor. Shamed, yet hoping to escape detection, I left the room walking backwards to hide the wet spot on my dress. I raced back to the camp without confrontation. Some days later, I was again ignored in my urgent need for the bathroom. This time, my desk-mate, a lively, bob-haired girl, noticed the suspicious little puddle under our seat and shrieked her discovery to the entire class. The next day, my mother was summoned to school and was to relay a message to me: 'Just go when you have to' – there would be no more waiting.

Perhaps to compensate for that shameful episode at school, I made a bold act of defiance. As Hanukkah, a post-biblical and primarily secular holiday approached, I resolved that we would treat it as a religious observance, with work forbidden in Orthodox tradition. I thought that the village school would not know the intricacies of Jewish festivals and, proceeding from that assumption, I assumed a rabbinic role, decreeing that we were on vacation. My camp friends neither questioned nor challenged this ruling, and we stayed home. As I was luxuriating in my freedom (Hanukkah being a commemoration of civic and religious liberty), one of the camp administrators stormed into my parents' room where I lay stretched out on their bed. In a rage, she demanded to know who gave me permission to sanctify this day. The following day we were back at school, our battle for self-determination lost. Audacious on my own terrain, I was forced into compliance in that other realm.

While my reputation at school was less than stellar, my stature at Beau Site was secure. In an evening's entertainment, 'amateur night at the camp', I performed a monologue, 'La Poupette'. My only props a kerchief on my head and a broom in my hand, I berated the lifeless doll before me, exhorting her to come to life, to come to my aid, and to help with my chores. With passionate voice and gestures I tried to rouse her. My parents had to be away from camp that day, but from the corner of my eye I recognized the schoolteacher in the audience. She had come to see my performance. The next morning, Mama told me that everyone raved to her about my presentation: 'Such courage, such confidence!'

Two years later, as a new immigrant in Boston, I would once again perform 'La Poupette'. Hoping to elevate the educational level of the school, the principal, a zealous Francophile, had put me on the spot; I couldn't refuse because he was my link to the language I'd spoken in public all my life. This time reciting the French poem to a group of bewildered children, I had no props, no enthusiastic audience; I had lost my theatre.

I learned to read in Morgins, but I became a reader in Clarens. For the first time, I acquired my own books, which replaced postage stamps as the vehicle for fantasy and exotic escapes. I delighted also in the illustrations of storybooks – a new experience, visual imagery, which up to then had been limited to my drawings and those of camp artists. *The Story of Ferdinand* by Monro Leaf was one of my favourites: the hero, a bull, true to his nature, who was happy to sit under a tree smelling the flowers, indifferent to fame, embodied qualities that captivated me, that I wished for myself; I saw in the book the championing of the rebel.

Reading offered not only the intrinsic joys of entering the world of imagination but also the gift of a new and unique friendship, one born of the exchange and discussion of books. This friend was a recent refugee whom I called Monsieur Souris (Mr Mouse, Mr Smiler) because our bond was established over the Mickey Mouse book I'd lent him after my first reading – we read every book several times. I was thrilled and surprised that he enjoyed the book as much as I did: an adult, but childlike in appreciating the spirit of mischievous little Mickey. Monsieur Souris moved like a spry little mouse, with quick energetic gestures. A small, sprightly, dark-haired man, with a trim moustache and expressive dark eyes, he always smiled at me, and joked with me – hence the pun on *souris* which I was old enough then to understand and apply. I don't recall his real name, but his essence is imprinted in my heart. He was my first adult friend, not in the impersonal, generic way friendship is often extended to children, but as a real pal, always ready for some fun.

Monsieur Souris's wedding was the first I'd ever attended. Everyone in the camp was present, witnessing and rejoicing in the couple's happiness. We knew that the bride had lost her entire family; I heard my parents say that this marriage was a new beginning, not only for them but for all Jews who had survived the Holocaust. They were a lovely pair, ethereal as they stood under the wedding canopy. She was blonde, with delicate features and a gentle, sweet aura about her. I knew her only as one of the adults, but I believe she was one of the Hungarian survivors who came to Switzerland close to the end of the war. During one part of the ceremony I saw some people weeping silently. I turned to my mother: 'I don't understand; if this is such a happy occasion, why are people crying?' Later, she explained to me that because bride and groom were orphaned, the '*Ayl Moley Rakhamim*' (Merciful God), a prayer in memory of their departed parents, was chanted during the wedding ceremony. I imagined their parents looking down on the couple from heaven, guests from above.

On that special day, I was dressed up in a white angora sweater (a hand-me-down, I assume, donated by a welfare organization). Standing in a circle of children, I felt like a kitten, lovingly stroked and held on a soft lap. And then, I glimpsed a little group of girls staring at me. 'Frieda, you look so nice today', they smirked and fussed. I understood their compliments were a thinly veiled commentary on my usual drab, makeshift garb. I saw myself as an imposter, hiding in the sensuality of my festive dress. I wanted to shed that ridiculous costume, to once again put on my overalls and join the boys who cared little for such display.

Relaxed rules about camp leaves brought new independence to our lives; moreover, we children now had new places to explore, foreign languages and unfamiliar sounds to discover. The diminutive bus stop in Morgins, a patch of worn gravel, was replaced by the spacious Montreux train station, with its promise of endless, interconnecting destinations and routes. After school, we would scamper down to the station along a road of glorious terraced vineyards. Had we been emissaries of the Swiss government we could not have been more fervent in greeting the frequent trains of American soldiers, who were then a presence in Europe. I can still see the slant of the late afternoon setting sun on the station platform, where we stood on tiptoe to reach the soldiers. Leaning out of the window during a stopover, the GIs laughed and joked with us, their mirth contagious. They charmed and amused us with their broken French, sending us into fits of giggles. To me they seemed to emanate from a wholly other universe. They threw packs of gum to us. We chewed this strange, magical treat that was not consumed, but like the burning bush retained its mass; then the champed wads went from mouth to mouth. No future confection would ever contain the sociability of that much travelled, rubbery gum, the signature of American soldiers in post-war Europe. At the time, it occurred to me that when we received our visas and came to America, I would have my own gum, sans chewing partners.

Decades later, I watched a film about Gertrude Stein: in one scene she is shown at the liberation of Paris, encircled by GIs; they are enchanted, enthralled by one another. We hear her rich voice declare that she can't get enough of their presence, of their talk, which speaks to her so vividly. That scene of such exuberance instantly brought me back to 1945, to the Montreux train station.

Was my experience of the end of the war, of the liberation of Europe, moderated and mediated by the grief around me? The war was over, but that historical event brought no end to sorrow. Indeed, for many it signalled the end of hope. For them the daily updated Red Cross and Jewish organizations' lists of survivors left only a void; the truth: no one was left. By late 1945, my mother would have known that her brother Herman, his wife Regina and their two children, Maxl and Susi, had perished in a concentration camp. Together, we had crossed the borders to Brussels and then France, but instead of coming with us to Lyon, as my parents had urged, they remained in a small village where they hoped they would be safe. From there they were deported. I have no recollection of my mother receiving that dreaded news. Like so many Holocaust survivors and refugees, my parents rarely spoke to me of their losses. Photographs of joyous occasions such as weddings or birthdays of grandchildren, taken years later in America, usually show my mother in a sad and distracted state as if she were remembering her dead relatives who should have been present at the celebration. At those same festivities, my father, who had also lost members of his family, is pictured in a more appropriate pose, present in the moment. A skilled dissembler, he often said life had taught him that grief concealed was the wiser course.

At that time, was I setting out on the romantic journey depicted in the *Bildungsroman*? Educational, developmental novels have always drawn and inspired me, especially when I was a university student who could recognize that genre. Was I following that literary path, leaving the village for a city of promises, replacing my parochial schooling with a liberal education? How and when do we know or recognize whether a particular moment has been a transition and/or a threshold? I was a transient in every sense except in my own consciousness: I now picture myself during that brief period, on a threshold to greater comprehension of my world, encouraged and stimulated by the surrounding social and geographic environment. In retrospect, so it appears to me, traits that would become permanent dispositions and patterns were then already perceptible. My impassioned prodding towards action in the monologue 'La Poupette'; my challenging the authorities and organizing classmates on Hanukkah; these inclinations would re-emerge decades later as I became an activist in the American peace movement and feminist politics. In embracing Clarens/Montreux as a liberation of sorts, was I turning my back on my Morgins past, my life in the Alpine shtetl, limited, homogeneous, but deeply rooted and familiar?

The lure of the larger, cosmopolitan world prefigured later years when I would flee the constraints of Boston and an over-protective family for emancipatory New York.

Waiting, the mark of refugee existence, took on meaning for me in Clarens. I knew that we would not be there for long; even we children were aware that permanent residence in Switzerland was denied to us. A Yiddish joke circulating in the camp highlighted the absoluteness of that policy: 'How can a refugee become a Swiss citizen? By dying and being reborn here; and even then, you can't be sure.'

In reading the refugee newspapers which emerged towards the end of the war, I recognize my family's predicament: they were among those who refused the return to Poland, their birthplace, or to Austria, their home since 1925. They were awaiting the visa to America for which they had applied in Vienna in 1938; the war, and the status of the Polish quotas, among the lowest on the list for immigration, had extended the waiting period.

I recall from those months after the war that we were also in line for migration to Palestine; 'whichever comes first' was our watchword. Had I been given a vote in the determinations, I would have elected Palestine, a country that had layers of meaning and affection for me. However, our chances were slight, since according to British criteria my parents and I were not considered high priority.

Zionists from their youth, my parents considered Palestine an authentic choice after the war. Papa had gone there for an exploratory visit in 1934, but returned to Vienna to resume a life which seemed then secure. An additional inducement, of course, was my brother Max's recent *aliyah* (migration) to Palestine. As a teenager who had been in a kibbutz preparatory programme, he had been in one of the first groups to emigrate. I can still see the crowd, eager for news and details, encircling my mother. Standing erect before the assembly, she held the thin tissue paper between her fingers and read aloud Max's first letter from Palestine. Hanging on to every word, they provided a stream of commentary after each line. I stood outside the group, inhaling the moment, conscious of the great pride I felt as Max's little sister. Uncertain of what was ahead, I was nevertheless excited by the prospect of foreign lands.

Journal Entry: 12 November 2001

Ruminations on the train back to Geneva from Clarens/Montreux:

I undertook that short trip without much enthusiasm, my expectations of the day modest, but since I was so near I decided to take a break from my research in the gloomy Geneva archives and enjoy a balmy autumn day in the environs I recalled as unalloyed beauty. Ambivalence and uncertainty characterized my approach to Clarens: on a trip to Switzerland in 1989, I'd been unable to locate our camp; after a futile bus ride, which I took as an omen, I gave up and consigned Clarens to the realm of the lost. More determined this time, I consulted the tourist bureau close to the Montreux train station; there I found a charming, helpful guide who understood within seconds what I was looking for when I told her that I had been a refugee.

A short bus ride later, I was walking up the incline leading to Beau Site. On that clear, bright day the hotel stood in bold relief, but the full force of recognition, of having been there before, came only when I walked around to the back and saw the terraced countryside. Fifty-six years had passed since I had been in that landscape. The autumn foliage was ripe with colour and the vegetable garden still had life and weight, tufts of green visible. The season of year corresponded with our arrival in 1945 and gave an uncanny flavour to the present moment: was I in the past or the present?

After introducing myself and my project to the amiable director of the residence, I was allowed to explore the ground floor on my own but asked to respect the privacy of the seniors' rooms upstairs. I was drawn immediately to the dining hall, unoccupied at the time, its wall of windows looking out on a luxuriant garden. The chairs and tables were arranged differently from how I recalled, less crowded, few traces of life. Was I expecting a room full of families, noisy children at mealtime? The past? I failed in my attempt at imaginatively animating the space before me, which remained lodged in the present, stubbornly resisting the reinstatement of a former life. It was here, in this very space, that I'd had my first theatrical exposure.

My steps quickened as I left Beau Site and headed for my old school. The walk up the hill, towards l'École Chantilly, I remembered so well: a sign now designated *Chemin des Ecoliers*, with the modern, universal symbol for children crossing; the stone wall and the embankment along which we three girls walked, where we conducted our quarrels or made up; chestnuts we used to gather, on the ground.

The principal's office was closed: only a concierge and a young teacher were in the school. Bad timing on my part: it was noon and no child was in sight. The classroom, once so severe, was bright, cheerful, full of colour. The windows were still the same, floor to ceiling, but gone was the pedestal for the *maîtresse*'s desk. The range of names on the pupils' drawings displayed on every wall was multicultural: another change from 1945, when we three refugee girls were nameless. I saw the girls' toilet which I had not reached in time and consequently had my 'accidents'.

In the early evening, on the train back to Geneva after my brief sojourn to Clarens, I felt strangely depleted. The day lacked the emotional tenor I had hoped for; I had not touched a nerve. The trip, nevertheless, recovered some aspect of my past, of my maturing self.

7

GENEVA: 1946

I first began to feel the outsider, the stranger, to feel the stigma and sting of being a refugee, during our last months in Switzerland. These months in 1946 returned us to Geneva, our first place of residence following our illegal crossing. My parents and I once again lived as a family, while my brother, in Palestine for almost a year, was settled in a kibbutz and playing in a soccer team. Behind us were three years of internment in two refugee camps, Morgins and Clarens. Now free to come and go (within reason and borders), we waited and readied ourselves for the voyage to America.

The war was over, but no trace of what should have been an unforgettable moment remains in my recollections. This continues to baffle: why would I forget that marker of time, while remembering so many less significant incidents of those years? Trying to account for that amnesia, I am left with conjecture only. What may have been a day of rejoicing for most of the world – with its iconic images of dancing in the streets, embracing Allied soldiers – was for Holocaust refugees, so many of them stateless, the start of yet another period of displacement: of waiting for their number to appear on the quota list for the desirable countries; of searching for an affidavit donor, then waiting again for the precious visa. Wandering, attempting to reconstruct a life, but with whom? The name of a parent, a spouse, a member of a once extended family, fails to appear on the constantly revised list of survivors. As children, would we have sensed the turmoil and calamity of 1945, that year when peace came to the world?

My own perception of the war's end takes on a transcendent nature. It avoids the worldly event and links it instead to a child's version of the world to come. Yiddish songs proclaiming the coming of the Messiah were sung with great conviction in the camps: one song, which still echoes in my mind, staged his arrival with a celebratory feast, at which Moses would teach us Torah, King David would play on his harp, and Miriam the prophet would dance for us. When would that day come? One day, walking up the hill in Morgins, arm in arm with my best friend Sorale, we predicted that the end of the war would be his appointed time, satisfied that we had settled the issue.

The war had now been over for almost a year but the Messiah tarried. This time, my parents and I were anticipating a more secular marker of redemption, our visas for the United States. The application process had been initiated in 1938 in Vienna, after the Anschluss, when it became clear that Austria was no longer safe for Jews. Foredoomed by the low Polish quota, my parents' visa was delayed for eight years (my parents were considered Polish nationals despite their twelve-year residence in Vienna); later, the war itself prevented migration to America. By now we were as impatient to leave this country of asylum as the Swiss were to see us move on. Refugee life could not end too soon in the land where fear of *Überfremdung* was elevated to policy: 'the lifeboat is full' accepted as realpolitik.

For the interval we rented a furnished room with a kitchen and toilet, from a dour, taciturn Swiss woman whose paraffin-wax pallor frightened me. Years later, her appearance came back to me when I read about Uriah Heap: bent over, skulking about. She was rarely present, but her room kept locked during her absence, confirmed our status as transients. The apartment was on the second floor of an antiquated house on Rue Beauregard, in the old quarter of Geneva. The front of the building, an unadorned, nineteenth-century facade, faced a broad, pleasant street, but for some reason (were we still hiding?) we always used the back entrance that looked onto a narrow, dark alley. It was from this dreary spot that like a bugler I would raise my head and shout 'Mama', every day when I returned home for lunch. My mother would lean out of the kitchen window, and only then did I enter the house. I remember that answering my call she often seemed breathless and red-faced, as though roused from another world. Was she reliving the past? Memories of life in Vienna before the Holocaust? Was it the loss of family that occupied her thoughts?

On a visit in 1989, the fiftieth anniversary of the start of the Second World War, hoping the occasion would soften all hearts, I knocked at the door of our old apartment on Rue Beauregard. An elderly woman cut from the same cloth as our former landlady stood guard at the entrance. In my rehearsed French I appealed to her: 'I was a refugee here during the war, and we lived here for a brief period. Please, can I just have a moment's look?' She slammed the door on my last syllable. Humiliated, I ran down the stairs, *l'esprit de l'escalier*, a venomous belated response seething inside me. Once outside, I caught a glimpse of a marker indicating that Franz Liszt had once lived on this same street; that link brought me inexplicable pleasure.

Shortly after we arrived in Geneva, my parents enrolled in a course sponsored by ORT (Organisation, Reconstruction, Travail), a Jewish vocational organization, training them to be knitting-machine operators, an exercise reflecting neither past experience nor their skills and proclivities. It did serve, however, to occupy them during this transition period and to satisfy the Swiss mania for busy hands, especially in Geneva, the birthplace of Calvinism. Thus, we became a family of students.

During those nine months in Geneva I attended l'École Malagnou, a short walk from our flat, down wide steps overarching an elegant boulevard. I was 8 years old when I entered Madame Meyar's second grade. A spacious, many-windowed classroom at street level adjoined a gleefully used, just-as-it-should-be playground. A year earlier Clarens had exposed me to Swiss public education, but that was in a small, rural setting, modest in comparison to this urban, sophisticated school near the University of Geneva. Now, for the fourth time in my childhood, I had to reconstruct myself, to make sense of events and people, to squeeze myself into the appropriate, required shape.

The more I sink back into that classroom of sixty years ago, the heavier my heart becomes. I was miserable there, friendless and bewildered by the school's procedures and conventions. Whatever our fate may have been in the refugee camps, there we were not the 'other'; we were all Jews in a closed and close community. Now, in this glorious, cosmopolitan city, I was the only Jewish child in the school. In retrospect, I realize that this was the first time in my life, and also the last, in which I would find myself in that singular position, unprepared for the lonely and isolating caste in Geneva.

Although my family led an observant Jewish life, had Jewish friends and even sent me to afternoon Hebrew school, l'École Malagnou was another matter entirely. From the start I stood out as the refugee. Most conspicuous was the clash of temporalities. Many Jews across the world, excluding those who live in large Jewish centres, recall the ordeal of school absences during Jewish holidays; mercifully, those days are distributed over the calendar year and, from one year to the next, we tend to forget our annual predicament. Switzerland offered no such respite for its Jewish minority: classes were in session on Saturdays, the Jewish Sabbath. This remains true even today – the Swiss schools take their break in the middle of the week. My parents, Orthodox Jews, were faced with a dilemma: writing is prohibited on the Sabbath, but weekly truancy was no solution. My parents would not have forced the issue, but I wanted to please them. So I went to school on Saturdays, dressed in my Sabbath outfit and sat at my nailed-down desk like an amputee, participating in the oral segments of the day, but avoiding any manual activity. What should have been a day to celebrate became a time to dread.

Nor was the Sabbath the only path to my pariah status at school: daily life, or *la vie quotidienne*, as it would have been referred to then in francophone Switzerland, offered countless reminders that I was the stranger in their midst. My classmates were little Swiss citizens: tidy, well-behaved, complacent if not smug. They embodied a sense of comfort and belonging in their world, while I was ill at ease, out of place, dropped into that universe by a catastrophic accident of history. So many of the school's activities showed me up as the intruder, inept in the ways of the Swiss. The commanding themes were neatness, orderliness, cleanliness and compliance; in all these qualities I failed. The routine in Madame Meyar's class began each morning by shaking our teacher's hand, accompanied by '*Bonjour, Madame*': this ritual took place even for latecomers, a category in which I often found myself. With every pupil watching, I would walk to the front of the class and wait until she was ready to receive my handshake and greeting, and only then could I retreat to my desk.

Hygiene preoccupied the Swiss, and the school in Geneva reflected that concern. Periodically we were examined for grooming and maintenance failures. Outbreaks of childhood diseases had been a constant reality in Morgins, and milder manifestations of communal living such as impetigo were ever present. Tincture of violet was the preferred treatment for this facial scab, and some child always bore that mark of camp life. I knew that in Geneva such bodily violations would not be so easily indulged.

One morning in the middle of the school year, Madame Mayer announced: 'Today, a nurse will be visiting our class on a health inspection.' No reason, no explanation, was given for this interruption in our usual routine. I was sitting at my desk in a dreamy state and didn't immediately grasp her message. And then, alarm: what happened? Why a health inspection now? What would it mean for me? What would the nurse be looking for? Would we have to undress? A vaccination maybe? I pictured a row of white uniformed nurses standing at the front of the room, needles in hand ready to prick our arms or, worse, our bottoms.

No escape seemed possible. Should I affect fainting? Perhaps I could sneak out undetected when I went to the toilet? These schemes were unlikely to succeed and might cause even greater problems than the health inspection. And what was I really afraid of? As these competing thoughts swirled through my mind, the door to our classroom opened.

One woman entered, not the army I'd imagined. She wore a dark blue skirt and white blouse, altogether ordinary-looking, all mediums: height, weight, hair colour and voice range.

Madame Meyar asked us to come to the front of the room in pairs, beginning with the front row. My seat was in the last row, allowing a temporary reprieve. I watched as Jacqueline, from the first row, presented herself. She showed no sign of fear or hesitation. I couldn't hear the instruction but I saw Jacqueline extend both hands, fingers spread, to the nurse. That simple gesture of showing her hands sent a current of panic through me. I had warts on both my thumbs. I pictured the scene when the nurse and the entire class would gasp in horror as they saw them. My row was called and as I stood in line waiting my turn, touching my little growths, trying to rub them out, an intervention from above: a voice spoke to me: 'Deliver only eight fingers, thumbs tucked under.' I descended the evolutionary ladder, and a rare moment of satisfaction swept over me as my pale growths went undetected and I passed inspection.

One particular instrument of quiet torment I recall in my bones even after sixty years. Early in the year we were handed a blindingly white cotton strip about twelve by thirty centimetres, along with a small spool of pink thread. We were instructed to practise making tiny and – for the very ambitious – invisible stitches. My Swiss classmates went about the task with zeal and skill, outdoing each other in animating this inert swathe with uniform, microscopic stitches, all the while maintaining the standard of cleanliness expected of us. My cloth was fingermarked at the first sitting, and my stitches, unruly and random, had an air of dissoluteness about them. Neither time nor effort improved my enterprise: my little piece just became greyer, more soiled and wrinkled with each sitting, the stitches more and more erratic. The finish of the school year brought a merciful end. To this day, that mistreated and bruised fabric has remained a reminder of my tenure at the l'École Malagnou. And to this day I loathe any kind of needle-and-thread interaction.

Poor eyesight was an additional contributor to my sense of displacement. The blackboard at the front of the class was always covered with arithmetic problems that were harder for me to read because of the mix of Arabic numerals and Roman letters. Misreading the exercises on the blackboard, I couldn't comprehend the questions, and this resulted at times in fantastical creations of my own: *moins* (minus) became *mains* (hands). In that configuration I see myself squinting through the glare on the slate surface at a blackboard full of hated numbers (all through my schooling, occasionally continuing into the present, I had a recurring nightmare: I enter a classroom and every wall is covered with blackboards and every blackboard is covered with math exercises, problems to be copied and solved, arrows shooting at me). The words were also my tormentors: what did *cinque mains trois* (five hands three) mean? I tried to decipher this cryptic language: five hands, so what? What was I supposed to do? I was afraid to disclose my ignorance to the teacher or to the other pupils.

Gone was the children's universe of the refugee camps. I'd been cast out of the Alpine shtetl, the kibbutz-like communal life of three years. These Genevese children in Madame Meyar's second grade didn't want me. The truth is, I did not belong in that bright classroom. Why? I was the stranger in their midst; and everyone knew it. I was foreign; to them my mother looked odd, comic. I was outside the circle and I couldn't enter. Was it because there were only girls in my class and I'd never been at ease with girls? Everyone had a buddy; I was alone, different, unwanted. I tried so hard to fit in, to whisper during class like everyone else who had a best friend, but no one wanted my messages. I longed to be like the other girls, to be part of the buzz, to join the cabal, arms draped around a confidante. I murmured to my desk-mate, Madeleine, a mate in name only; she ignored me, ridiculous figure that I must have seemed.

But speech came at a cost: '*Babil*' and '*Babillarde*' (chatterbox, prattler), appeared almost weekly under '*deportment*' in my report card. *Babil* reduced to babble my attempts at belonging. Alone in my mind but judged guilty of prattle. It is Saturday: my parents and I are seated at the kitchen table for our Sabbath meal. I hand Papa my report card with its stiff Van Gogh sunflower-yellow cover and wait; the opening page reveals my low grade, a four in '*deportment*' with the comment, *Babillarde*. My father may not know enough French to catch its meaning but he certainly understands my shamefully low grade in conduct. His usually glad face darkens into disappointment. I am used to his gaze filled with love and pride. Instead I sit by his side at the table and receive his scolding, though I sense that his reproach is motivated by propriety rather than conviction, that my low mark did not really worry my parents; perhaps it secretly pleased them that I had not been silenced.

Had I accepted the isolation, the mark of outsider; had I held my tongue and acquiesced, perhaps turning it into a virtue, becoming the taciturn observer, watching, noting their ways, keeping my thoughts to myself; had I assumed that role, I would at least have held onto my dignity. I would have kept myself hidden from them, kept from them all clues to who I was. But no: I rejected dignified silence and hurled my way into their circle, where I remained uninvited. I persisted, deepening the pain of exclusion by my own response and behaviour. '*Babillarde*': had I deserved the label, had it pointed to a lively sociability, the popular girl in the class, who can't contain her exuberance and risks punishment, who deserves the label, but to be called 'chatterbox' when I knew so well (as my teacher must have also known) that there was no one who wanted to receive my talk, I was a speaker without an audience.

My glasses, of little help where it mattered, reading the lessons on the blackboard, contributed greatly to my self-consciousness. One day, as we stood in line, about to be dismissed, a very pretty and therefore popular girl – I think her name was Jaqueline – rose above us, announcing that she was about to examine our glasses and hand down her judgement. Methodically, she scrutinized every spectacled girl. I felt she was including the wearer as well in her rating system: some were beautiful, others less so. Then she turned her sharp little eyes on me and my very plain glasses: 'Frieda's glasses are ugly, *laid*, the ugliest in the class.' She emphasized every syllable in that short, brutal sentence. So many French words have been forgotten; *laid* is imprinted.

Although I had no friends among my classmates, there was one kindred spirit, another outcast: her misfortune was divorced parents. I ran into her and her mother once on a busy street in Geneva and she greeted me like an old pal. That is the only recollection I have of an amicable exchange with someone my own age from l'École Malagnou.

One afternoon, walking home alone, climbing the steep incline towards my house, I heard a group of older girls laughing at me; their words have left me, but their taunts and threatening behaviour remain. They hurled their leather book-bags at me and I ran the rest of the way home. When I told my father about the incident, he gave me a knowing look; we both understood that this was inevitable.

Close to the end of the school year, in June 1946, our class went on a boat ride on Lake Geneva. I recall the sun reflected on the lake. I stayed close to Madame Meyar who was with a friend. Both women made me feel welcome in their company, but why was I not with the other children, why was I with the teacher? I took along my crocheting (working on a shoulder bag, popular in those days, in blue and green wool) and I went at it fiercely, lifting the wool onto the crochet needle, piercing the circumference, stabbing the air until the yarn and needle met. (Although I avoided sewing whenever possible, mistakes could easily be concealed in crocheting.) I recall the water, the sun, the sky, the boat, my teacher and her companion and my crocheting, but no friend in sight. Where were all the classmates? In my memories of the boat excursion I am a child behaving like an adult with her crocheted bag and her adult interlocutors. All the wonderful things offered: the boat trip, the lavish celebration of promotion day: in all those, I'm alone.

Not only was I the quintessential foreigner, but if I had any notion of trying to conceal that stigma, my mother's presence ensured that I would remain who I was. In the refugee camps there had been mothers whose contact with reality – do we even know what that may have been then? – had been deeply disturbed; some went mad – not really violent, but we knew who they were. My mother did not fit that pathological category, nor was she amongst those mothers who presented themselves to the world as highly functioning, and I knew that. In the calmer and more conventional environment of Geneva, her eccentricity, which had been muted compared to the extremes around her in the camps, now took on a more flamboyant expression.

Picking me up after school on some days, she would wear outrageous costumes, whatever came to hand, I suppose: a turban, trousers, a trench coat. By contrast, the Swiss mothers blended into the background as they stood in their well-fitting clothes, self-contained beings, waiting serenely for their daughters to run into their arms. My mother paced nervously while she waited for me to emerge from the classroom. Was it a deep shame or a momentary embarrassment that made me pull her away from the schoolyard and head for home?

What now remains of those school days? When I pick up my grandchildren after school, I am full of dread, apprehension in my every step. As it was in Geneva in 1946, here too, among the parents, grandparents and nannies, some are jolly, effusive, as they watch for their children, others stand grim and anxious. So it was with my children and so it continues with my grandchildren. I sometimes forget who I am and where I am; I become both my mother and the child I was. Geneva, New York, Toronto: the essential experience repeats.

Mama faced the danger of a little learning with equanimity; she was undaunted by the difficulties she encountered daily in a country which, at best, tolerated her. Practised in the art of defiance, her camp experience having provided her with a large canvas, now in Geneva she challenged the authority of the French Academy, guardians of the French language. Forging ahead, she replaced Yiddish, our lingua franca in Morgins and Clarens, with *la langue française*. Disregarding with utter abandon all rules of grammar and syntax, treating vocabulary as an annoying convention, she refused to be silenced, although I wouldn't let her talk in public when we were together. Years later, when we were in Boston, my mother insisted on speaking to me in French whenever we were somewhere within earshot of people; the subway was her favourite venue. At those times, I would pretend that I didn't know her. The outcome of my youthful arrogance was that I forgot my French soon after embracing English; my mother retained her knowledge of the language, however imperfect, for the rest of her life.

Less than a decade later, I was 17, a waitress at a summer resort in Maine, on my own for the first time. Caroline, another summer worker, entered my life. She was beautiful, a head taller and two years older than I: a flamboyant art student while I was still at the strict, repressive Girls' Latin School. An unlikely match for a friendship, we were nonetheless drawn to each other that summer at the Lafayette family resort in Old Orchard Beach. Our bond continued when we returned to our regular lives in Boston.

I was anxious about Caroline's first visit to my house. What would she think of my parents, their immigrant ways, their halting English, their European manners? As she was leaving, my sophisticated friend whispered to me: 'Your mother is fabulous, Frieda. She's a real bohemian; I love the way she talks and looks. You're so lucky.' That day opened the path to shifting perceptions; I began to see my mother in another light: respected, cherished for her unconventional ways, admired for her quirky intelligence, her highly-honed moral imagination. That realization, that new insight, in time redeemed me too. Gradually I took up the mantle of bohemianism, a word I rarely hear today, but which in the 1950s gave me entry to a wider, more liberal and diverse universe. And Amelia (Malice was her Jewish name), my mother, became my model as I moved toward adulthood and motherhood. Some of her traits that had made my childhood in Switzerland such a complicated and troubling terrain were the very ones which in later years contributed to my independence and tenacity.

I look back and remember: my mother never said 'no' to me. Unaware that parents were meant to discipline their children, or perhaps disdaining that role, she never exerted blind authority over me. She brought me breakfast in bed on Saturdays and allowed me to stay home from school whenever I had a painful menstrual period. Her slanted perspective reshaped the world for me; shorter by a few inches than I, she looked up to me as a giant. 'You have such broad shoulders, and you are tall just like Papa', she would say with pleasure in her offspring. It was only in my teens that I looked around and noted that I was among the petite ones in most groups of girls.

I attended private Hebrew classes several afternoons and Sunday mornings at Suzanne's home which I seem to recall was an apartment-hotel. Our teacher, a dark-haired, handsome young man, embodied a bored, *je-ne-sais-quoi* manner: teaching elementary Hebrew to young girls was not what destiny had intended for him. Our lessons were *haymish*, homey; we could speak freely, few rules fettering our lively spirits. I was on familiar, happy ground, the foundation for my Jewish education having been laid in Morgins. Additional enticement came from knowing that my brother was speaking that ancient language in his new country, that he was kicking a soccer ball in Hebrew, working at his gardening job *b'Ivrit* (in Hebrew). I often felt his presence when I read or stumbled over a word.

Suzanne was my only real friend in Geneva. Lithe and tall, she resembled her young, glamorous, French-born mother. Unlike the more controlled curls of the day, Suzanne's golden-brown hair had a natural swing to it; it flew in all directions when she gestured a sentence. We were opposites in appearance and family background: my parents, middle-aged, traditional Jews had lived in Vienna for over a decade, but the Polish air still clung to them. Suzanne, full of mirth, shared a mischievous disposition with me. Nudges and pinches drew our attention to a moment we couldn't let pass; suppressed giggles were our private language. Occasionally Suzanne's mother would appear during class time, her presence lending an aura of excitement to the hour because we were old enough to recognize the signs of attraction in the conspiratorial glances exchanged between her and our teacher.

I still have the thin prayer book, *Nos Principal Prières*, with its yellowed, brittle pages and blue cover. The former owner's name in fine script appears inside the front page and in my own less elegant handwriting: Frieda Johles, *Hebreu*. The bilingual (French and Hebrew) text begins with the Morning Prayer for children, '*Modeh Ani*', in which we thank God for returning our soul to us. Decades later, as a student of Yiddish at Oxford, I heard a young Frenchman chanting that prayer in a melody I still carry with me.

My hair was always my undoing. In an era when curls were what the well-dressed girls wore, I had straight, stubborn hair. There was little doubt in my mind as to which had greater cachet: curls gave you an immediate advantage over those with straight hair, whether braided or hanging loose, whether in cosmopolitan Geneva or provincial Morgins. A curly head gave you a sense of being blessed, of nature singling you out.

My mother had neither talent nor patience for elaborate hairdos. I eventually became very proficient at hair styling, but at the age of 8 or 9 I still depended on the adults in my life. Occasionally, Elfi, the teenage daughter of distant relatives, would come over to try her hand at turning my listless head of hair into a coiffure with bounce and verve. Rag curls, which she tried so hard to introduce, never held for more than half an hour. She even tried waxed toilet paper on which the hair was rolled, the end moistened with water or saliva, depending on the refinement of the hairdresser.

The last day of the school year was celebrated throughout Geneva, a children's holiday with all the fanfare of a national festival. All of Geneva's schoolchildren gathered in the luxurious municipal hall to receive their certificates of promotion to the next grade. My mother took this uniquely Swiss occasion very much to heart, as though she were a fifth-generation Genevan; I did not share her enthusiasm nor her sense of inclusion. But metaphysics notwithstanding, I agonized about my appearance, especially my hair. I knew that even Elfi couldn't make the curls last long enough to see me through the elaborate ceremony. I devised an ingenious but pathetic solution: I tied very thin light-brown thread (the natural colour of my hair) around the ends of my hair. I probably looked ridiculous but what I remember most vividly of that day was joyously walking with the sun behind me casting a shadow on what looked like a head of swinging curls.

As the time of our departure drew near, the question of hairdos took on a more urgent tone: we were going to America and looking like refugees would not do. Discussions about the necessary alterations that were to take place did not include my father, who was well groomed, neatly dressed and could fit into any gathering. Mama and I needed a fundamental conversion in making the transition from refugee to immigrant status, the latter a step up in the calculation of the displaced. We were both marked by hair that gave us away immediately: I, at best, looked like a country girl with braids, while Mama, in coils severely pulled back from her thin face, revealed the austerity of her refugee days. The solution to our hair problems was permanent waves for both of us. And so Mama and I began our transformation together; we went to the same beauty salon and (to no one's surprise) left with identical hairdos. The tops of our heads, which should have been full of lovely ringlets framing our faces, were instead flat, in every sense of that word; the curls began midway down and went straight out, giving us a strangely wild look.

We now had another reason to cover our heads, which we would have to do in any case to be well dressed. Our misbegotten hairdos had to be kept under our hats. We walked out of the milliner's with our brown felts, with rolled-up brims and rounded crowns: mine had a smaller circumference but was otherwise identical to Mama's. In less than an hour I had turned into a middle-aged woman.

Those nine months in Geneva stand out in bold relief, corresponding in themes and meaning to the Jewish holidays that framed our lives. The holidays observed during the years of internment are blurry traces, shadowy memories. In part the haziness is due to my age: I was too young in the camps to have absorbed and integrated all the events around me. In Geneva, as we awaited our visa to America, festivals took on a distinct meaning: it seemed to me we were following a biblical script, and our lives and journeys were the stage on which it all played out.

Passover or Pesach – the Spring festival commemorating the exodus of the Israelites from slavery in Egypt, known as the time of our freedom – was the first I recall celebrating as a family unit. Shaped by my father's culinary magic, preparations for this elaborate holiday began with the live fish he brought home to our diminutive kitchen. The carp were released into a metal tub (the same one in which I took my weekly bath) where they would swim away their last laps.

That year, during Passover, Tante Rosa and Fritzi came from Zurich to spend the week with us. We knew that we would soon part ways and it might be years before we'd see one another again. Today, at 70, Fritzi still remembers the little fish in the leaden tub. Mrs Eisenstab and Elfi also joined our table for the Seder (the festive meal and accompanying Exodus story). As the youngest participant, I was designated to ask the 'Four Questions', the *Mah Nishtanah* (why is this night different from all other nights?). Papa led us in reading and singing the reply to that question found in the Hagadah, the text of the Seder.

Yom Kippur, the holiest day in the Jewish calendar, a Day of Atonement, fasting and prayer, coincidently brought us our ticket out of refugee land. Too young to fast for more than a few hours, I went home for lunch, while my parents stayed at synagogue the entire day. I hurried through the solitary meal Mama had left for me before she set out that morning. As I passed our mailbox on my way back, I saw a white envelope: I recognized the sender, the American consulate. I ran to *shul*, hoping, guessing that it was the long-awaited visa I was carrying. Papa, who was deep in prayer, would not even look at the envelope I held up to him. Mama, in the women's section in the balcony, saw me, and sensing that something was astir, beckoned to me. I rushed upstairs to her and she took the stuffed envelope without any hesitation. My parents would not open the envelope, as this would be considered work and was thus forbidden on this holy, awesome day. I, a child, with few religious restrictions, tore it open and revealed its contents: the visa to America.

I associate that Day of Atonement with a greater and more enduring gift than the arrival of our visa. It was the first of many Yom Kippur days that Mama and I would sit close to one another in synagogue, closer in spirit than at any other time. I see her still, with the special High Holy Days prayer book, the *Makhzor*, in her hand, in what the philosopher Martin Buber describes as a dialogue with God. Mama weeps silently, as do most of the women seated around her, when they recite the Memorial Service for their departed. And in 1946, in Geneva, everyone's memory was pierced by recent tragedy, neither fully assimilated nor belonging to the past. Years later, I marvelled at her continued faith in a personal God who intervenes in human affairs: continued after the Holocaust, after losing most of her extended family. Every Yom Kippur, I feel my mother sitting beside me at synagogue.

The festival that followed, Succoth – the holiday of huts, recalling the Israelites' nomadic years in the desert before entering the promised land – we celebrated in the knowledge that our days as wandering Jews were soon coming to an end; that link to the past, its significance to our own lives, was not lost on us.

When I recount my months in Geneva to friends, they sigh and fall silent; their eyes well up with tears. I am bewildered by their responses.

'What's wrong? What did I say?'

'You had such an unhappy, such a darkened childhood', they answer in hushed tones.

'A Dickensian childhood, or worse, is not what I intended to portray.'

They look baffled by my outcry. I want to say, 'Don't strip me of all I've worked so hard to achieve.' But I don't; I know they mean well, that they want to show sympathy and compassion for my early years during the war. But their well-intentioned words sound too much like pity, and in that instant their kind, caressing faces hurl me back to all the places where 'little refugee girl' was my epithet, where pity became my humiliation.

What could account for this discrepancy? Do my friends understand me better than I understand myself? Do they see that beneath the patina I'm still a refugee? Are they comparing their normal childhood complaints with mine? Perhaps they think that while an unhappy childhood may have been their lot too, it wasn't due to the catastrophe that surrounded me. But intimates are not the only ones to interpret my story in that light; people who know my history only in passing make the same judgement.

As I reassemble my experience in Geneva during those months, I see myself as contented, if not happy, when out of school, when I was out in the city. I protest to my friends: 'But that's not the whole picture; that's not what I'm left with when I recall those days in Geneva, when I was 8 and 9 years old.' I begin to explain: 'Don't forget, I was with my parents, doting and indulgent; I was the centre of their lives. It was the three of us against the world. You could say we were a triumvirate, without the attendant powers.' I pause, remembering my parents' loving gaze, their unreserved affection.

'I loved Geneva for what it gave me, for the beauty that surrounded and enveloped me at every turn. I inhaled its loveliness with every breath, sweetening the bitter taste of school. Everywhere nature and art collaborated; luxuriant parks on Lake Geneva, Mont Blanc in the background; streets and alleys well supplied with surprises, rising, dropping; cobblestoned squares in the cramped, old city; wide, bright, avenues in the newer part of town; open boulevards, grand nineteenth-century architecture, and magnificent bridges from one section of the city to another, which I crossed so often. Geneva remains in my pores as a city that did not hide from me, a blessing that was conferred on my childhood. Was I too young to absorb that generous, varied loveliness? I think not.

'In every city where my parents found themselves, they discovered the nearest park, abounding in arboreal splendour lavishly designed, or left for nature to take its course. Parks became our second home, especially for my mother, who bloomed in that setting. Like so many European parents, they valued the salubrious effects of fresh air, *gute Luft*: they spoke of it as good air. I recall only sunny skies, zephyrs on my cheeks.

'My eyes, my betrayers in the classroom, were free to alight on these glorious sights, and in those moments, they displaced the inner sense of failure, of rejection. In the open, I belonged to myself, no longer the stranger. No expectations or disappointments; no need to labour in the fields of attempted, spurned friendships, nor to struggle with the baffling requirements of school. Juxtaposed in my memory, Geneva is dominated by these competing realities.'

The moment I finish my monologue, I am overtaken by remorse. I have no moral right to utter the words 'beauty' and 'freedom ' in the context of the Holocaust. Beauty amidst horror and brutality: I think of Friedl Dicker-Brandeis, the gifted and highly respected Bauhaus artist who was deported to Theresienstadt. In that concentration camp where thousands died of starvation, disease and overwork, she held art classes for the children. Dicker-Brandeis was a serious teacher, encouraging and inspiring her young students to document their reality in drawings, watercolours, collage. In 1944 she was sent to Auschwitz, where she perished.

My Geneva in 1946: the war was over, our survival assured, how could I so blithely mix ethics with aesthetics! The painful school experience gave me some legitimacy. Yes, I may not have been in a concentration camp, but I too suffered. Yet when people react with 'poor child, lonely, ostracized' to descriptions of my childhood, I feel duplicitous in submerging the more complex in favour of more acceptable, more easily received layers. I'm quick to redirect them: I don't want their pity, applied so generously and, to my mind, so indiscriminately. I move back and forth trying to claim a place for myself; I acknowledge that I was isolated in that Swiss school, but that's not it. I demand the full truth, that my pain always be considered in relative terms, never in absolutes. At the same time I reject the smug posture of the lucky one. Underlying declarations of fortune's fickleness, I often hear a quiet voice that suggests the just dessert.

Addressing these categories of my life, fraught with confusion, disparate longings and often contradictory perceptions, I lose, for that moment, my hard-won status as citizen of the world, peace activist, feminist. I wish for comprehension, for moral imagination. The remarks of my friends are too close to the community centre stage where I was ordered to stand and listen as my benefactors referred to me as 'the little refugee girl from Hitler'. My friends have no way of knowing that their emotional response will set off an alarm in me. I also know that I bear some responsibility for their impression. I have often enmeshed my experience in irony, understatement or humour, attempting the amusing tale instead of what they want: the standardized show of feelings to accompany the customary picture of the Holocaust. I don't want to be consumed, swallowed up by their pity, nor do I want to be dismissed entirely as a fortunate survivor because I didn't suffer the ultimate tragedy. I want affection for the little girl I was; I want the link to the past but within my control, my direction. Once we arrived in America, I had little power to influence the monolithic perception that relatives, teachers, and classmates had of me. Boston, where we moved after a brief stay in New York, had few refugee children at that time and so Jewish organizations and schools made frequent use of our talents: we were brought out on celebratory holidays as well as on the frequent memorial occasions.

Moved by desperation not to be singled out, not to be spoken about as a fixed object destined to be a refugee in perpetuity, I learned English with astonishing speed: in six months I was fluent. Despite my success at shedding my French accent, of purging myself of the mark of foreigner, I could never be sure that my past was safely locked away.

On one occasion, a small group of us, sixth-grade girls, stood lined up, soldier-rigid, in the schoolyard facing the old brick building of our Jewish day school (I attended the Maimonides Educational Institute – a pretentious name for a very unpretentious school – for three years after we settled in Boston). Mrs Kirschen, our teacher, was the presiding judge, reprimanding us for bullying our more timid classmates. She was a large woman, with a voice that could make us tremble when she turned her anger on us. After enumerating our crimes, she turned her full body, flushed face, bulging eyes, heaving chest towards me. Up to that moment, I had felt myself part of the group, even enjoying the limelight. Then with panting breath, she said: 'Frieda Johles, you are the ringleader. We took you in when you came as a refugee, we were kind to you, and this is how you repay us. Shame on you.' I stared straight ahead, hatred for her filling every part of my being: not for singling me out as the ringleader – a role I secretly nurtured – but for resurrecting my history, which had lain dormant for the last few years. She remembered. My English, by then indistinguishable from my American classmates, did not protect me.

Several years later, at Girls' Latin School in Boston, where I thought my past would not follow me, I had another scare. Miss Cushing, my seventh-grade homeroom teacher, was also our geography teacher. One morning, reviewing an assignment on the European continent, she casually asked whether anyone in the class had ever been to Europe. I knew that she knew, through my school records, that I was born in Vienna. Miss Cushing looked around: no hand went up in answer to her question. She waited a minute, then slowly turned her back to us, her long pointer fixed on the wall-sized map of Europe and continued the lesson. Not until university was I released from the fear of exposure. Only in the safety and anonymity of that universe was I able to escape.

8

GENOA: 1946

In late November 1946, my parents and I left Switzerland for Italy, for Genoa, its largest port city, there to await our ship to America. We were going to New York, where my father's family, our sponsors, our affidavit donors, lived. Throughout the war, Papa's sister Regina and her husband Isaac had shared their modest immigrants' income with us; sending universally accepted dollars meant we were not totally dependent on charity. Throughout the war the proverbial 'Uncle in America' was our security, our symbol of possibility. Present in our lives, a helpline across the ocean, they would not abandon us. We were not alone. Few refugees were as fortunate. New York, with its reputation as a cosmopolitan centre, further heightened our anticipation. Taking on the responsibility of affidavit donor was no small matter, it was the linchpin in the immigration process. The donor had to guarantee that the immigrant would not become a ward of the state.

My parents had been in Genoa for barely a week when they received a visit from Rabbi Klein, who had been one of my favourite teachers in the Morgins camp. He came to plead: his family's visa would expire in two weeks and if they didn't sail within that period, they would be forced to reapply, a process taking months, perhaps longer. Adding to Rabbi Klein's predicament was his wife's illness. I recall seeing her in Morgins; her pallid face and halting gait expressed a tenuous link to life.

Would my parents exchange tickets with them? We could afford to wait since our visa had a later expiry date. It meant, however, that we would have to stay in Genoa for an additional month, waiting for the next boat. We see here a multilayered predicament involving class, status, ethics and, most central, the context in which this took place. To begin, Rabbi Klein was a respected teacher, scholar and religious leader in the camp community, who had served a prestigious congregation in Berlin before the war. My parents had owned a grocery/delicatessen in Vienna.

I was in our room when this drama unfolded. Slender, elegant, a trim, rabbinic beard, the rabbi carried himself with great dignity His oratorial gifts were eloquent yet modest in delivery. My parents stood in silence as he presented to them his request. My parents looked at each other; I turned from one to the other, searching for signs of their decision. My father nodded assent. Without a word passing between them, my parents granted the rabbi's request. I knew from the start they would not refuse him. How could they? Compared to the many risks and life-and-death decisions they had faced in the last eight years, this was another delay but not life-threatening. And yet, postponing the sea crossing during these unpredictable post-war years was more than mere inconvenience. It meant staying another month in considerable discomfort and displacement, especially for my ailing mother.

Looking back on those days in 1946, I realize how that act of exchanging ship tickets was uniquely a post-war experience coloured by the Holocaust. How could my parents have denied another survivor a safe passage when it was in their power to do so. In their view, I am certain, it was the only decent thing to do. While details differ, I now see the chain unbroken: my relatives in New York giving to us, and my parents' gift to the Klein family.

The rabbi's daughter, Sorale, had been my best friend in Morgins and I wanted her family's wish to be granted, but I also wanted to be in America to start our new life in New York, a city with enticing testimonials. With conflicting emotions about our delay to America, I nevertheless felt pride and satisfaction; my parents were now benefactors, a shift from being refugees who were beholden to others. In a heartless world, they stood by the principles that had been their heritage, a generosity that had informed all their acts. Their ethical stance then, and in years to come, shaped my own understanding of what it means to be human.

While at the Zurich archives, I came across documentation of the ticket exchange between the Johles family and the Klein family. Once again, my memory of that event was confirmed.

Switzerland and post-war Italy were a study in contrasts, a chiaroscuro of sorts. Dark, cold and grimy, Genoa still held the smell and taint of war. Less than a day's journey by train, it embodied war-worn Europe, while Geneva, the beneficiary of neutrality, had retained its lustre of peacetime prosperity.

Our *pension* housed a dozen or so Jews who had survived the Holocaust; some had been hidden in Italy, others had arrived after the war and were in transit to another country, just as we were. We were not among the gainfully employed, and this left many hours in the day for visits. The *pension* was a brief return to the communal life of the camps where we had shared a common fate. In our musty room, I was an avid listener to the conversations, discussions and communion taking place around me as callers – other residents – exposed parts of their life stories: where they had been, how they had survived and, so often, who had been lost. Some stood back from their own tragedy, analyzing events: which countries collaborated zealously with the Germans (Poland and France among the guiltiest), which people came to the aid of their compatriots and did not denounce their neighbours to the Nazis. In that *pension* in Genoa, in 1946, all agreed that the Italian population had been among the most humane to the Jews in their midst.

I was the only child in our *pension*, an arrangement I accepted as natural. I'd lost the child's world in Geneva, where I'd had only one friend. I grew accustomed to being my parents' companion. My parents did not – could not – shelter me from the revelations that were commonplace in the *pension*. Moreover, my presence at all times was also taken as normal by the adults in the *pension*. By then I'd already lived as my parents' companion in an adult world. Although I was not a participant, I was never bored by adults' conversations; I was drawn into them by my own curiosity.

An older woman who had befriended my parents told of her years in hiding. Her demeanour suggested a refinement and civility that even the severest calamity had not obliterated. 'The Italians', she said in a soft, but firm voice, 'did not round up Jews to send them to their deaths, the way other countries did. Many shared what they had with their Jewish friends at a time when there was little to share.' She paused, 'They saved my life; I'll never forget them.'

Years later, in my interview with a former refugee, I heard a similar testimony. Michel recounted his years in a seminary in the Italian sector of Switzerland:

> The brothers, priests, were wonderful to me; they treated me like an honoured guest, favouring me over the Christian boys at the school. For example, when I was in a fight during recess, if I was winning the brothers looked away; if I was on the losing end, they intervened and stopped the scuffle. In the summers when all the other boys went home, I remained and became a kind of member of the brotherhood; they took me with them wherever they went and that included wine-making; I even got drunk once.

Amidst the adversity, privation, and pervasive wretchedness that existed at the time, the Italians – shopkeepers, people on the street –

displayed warmth and compassion to us wherever we went. The owner of the restaurant where we took our daily meals greeted us like friends rather than refugees. Even as a child, I sensed the difference between their sociability, their openness, and the tight-lipped correctness of the Swiss.

It was in Genoa that I first heard detailed accounts of the Holocaust. I was 9 years old and knew about the war and about Hitler, but until then, it had been more or less an abstraction. I understood that over there, terrible events had taken place; I also remembered that some of my friends in Morgins and Clarens had lost their fathers. Now, I heard survivors tell their tragic stories. I assume that in my presence they refrained from expressing the unspeakable, particularities I was to learn later in America. How did I respond to those encounters in our small room? I have no vivid recollections; I merely see myself sitting under a blanket, listening.

A woman in her thirties was a frequent visitor to our room. She was a dark-haired beauty, with serious, deep blue eyes and a fine, fair complexion, but she had lost all vestiges of youth. She was especially friendly towards me, her eyes searching and meeting mine, engaging me in conversation; in her presence I was part of the group, not relegated to being the silent child among adults. One very cold afternoon, sitting on our bed, she told her story. She had been deported to a concentration camp with her husband and son; they had not survived. She told not only of her experience in the camps but also of life before the war: of her son, who used to fold his trousers every night and place them under his pillow to press them while he slept. In a calm, evenly modulated voice, with every now and then even a tiny smile, she recalled his nightly routine. That image has stayed with me: a young boy, no longer alive, who folded his pants methodically before sleep every night. I thought of my brother who was in Palestine.

During that clammy December, my mother's poor health kept her in bed much of the time. I spent most days with my father walking up and down the maze of bleak, narrow streets and medieval alleyways, which despite their shabbiness were hubs of urban life. I remember one scene because of my dramatic role in it. One of the side streets led us into an open square, with more light falling on it, the grey winter sky lifting. It was a place of some activity; in the centre, men sat at a makeshift table rolling dice. Papa wanted to join in the modest game, but I urged him not to gamble. I was the cautious one, afraid he would lose his money, and he deferred to me. It turned out that had he played as he wished, he would have won. Now, I can't recall how he could have known that possibility, but I do remember that he was quietly angry with me, disappointed and disapproving, and I wished I'd kept my thoughts to myself.

Toward the end of the month, we were summoned to the American consulate for the final medical examination prior to boarding ship. Suffering from lumbago and in constant pain, Mama bent forward, unable to straighten her back. She knew that were she to enter the examination room hunched over, the exit pass would not be granted. I saw her biting her lips, coaxing her spine into a vertical position. The examiner was a mild-mannered, distracted doctor who barely looked up from the forms he was completing. He passed us. Relief was all I felt at that moment, afraid to express joy, excitement or anticipation.

A landlocked childhood to a storm-ridden voyage: the smooth, tranquil waters of Lake Geneva had not prepared me for the sea we would cross on the old, war-weary Greek ship, *Katoomba*. My introduction to the oceanic universe had come through the movies, which were severely restricted in Switzerland, most films rated unsuitable for children. Would that the *Katoomba*'s sea-worthiness had been checked as rigorously; it sank soon after our voyage. One of the few films to meet the stringent criteria was a seafaring saga. On that rare, much awaited occasion in Geneva, I was among the excited audience for whom a darkened theatre held great promise. Once the titles were completed, the entire screen was covered in water; I didn't know at the time what an ocean was and, sitting in my seat, I thought that at any moment the waves would pour out of the screen and swallow me up. I grabbed my mother's hand, hid my face in her lap while she tried to calm my fears; her words were not convincing. I made no link between this and the real world, unaware that in less than a year this vastness of water would hold me for more than a month.

In late December 1946 we boarded the *Katoomba*, which was packed to the rafters with hundreds of displaced persons. Space was a luxury on the ship, and I was a movable entity. Since the women's dormitory had no bed for me, I was assigned to the men's section with my father. Among the crowd who shared Papa's dormitory were numerous Greek Orthodox priests who were high-spirited and remarkably solicitous towards me. Never before had I seen men of that religious faith: their cylindrical hats, long black robes and full beards enthralled me. I don't recall any self-consciousness in being the only female among scores of men. The many priests created a religious mood on ship, but since they were also family men, the patriarchal air was lightened.

Our Atlantic voyage in December/January was tempestuous; we felt endangered, this time by natural forces. Elderly Greek women immersed a wooden cross in a glass of water: if the cross sank, so would our ship, they predicted. Fortunately, the wooden cross floated and our safe crossing was assured. I never doubted their predictive powers. During a violent storm, when I fell against a lower bunk, these same women tended my sprained ankle with such tenderness: compresses, egg-soaked towels, were wrapped around my swollen ankle and by the time we disembarked, I could walk off the ship with no trace of an injury.

A transition it certainly was, and I felt that this was the end of my cosmopolitan existence: no longer would I hear such a gathering of languages: Greek, Yiddish, French: I was going to an English-speaking country where no one would understand me. I cannot account for the feeling, but I sensed that I was leaving behind a varied, multicoloured world and entering a monotonic future.

Central to my many-tiered, sometimes confused, memoir is the urgency I feel to preserve and protect this history, to have it stand as one of the testimonies of the period. In the next decades, few if any refugees of the Holocaust will be alive to tell that story from a child's perspective. Filtered through memory to be sure, but as authentic as we will ever have.

BIBLIOGRAPHY

ARCHIVES AND LIBRARIES

American Jewish Joint Distribution Committee Archives, New York.
Archiv für Zeitgeschichte, Eidgenössische Technische Hochschule, Zürich (Archives for Contemporary History, Zurich).
Archives of the Verband Schweiz Jüdischer Flüchtlingshilfen (VSJF) JUNA-Archiv.
BSJF-Archiv.
SIG-Archiv.
Nachlass Otto Zaugg.
Nachlass Gertrud Kurz.
Nachlass Samuel W. Jean Richard.
Nachlass Liselotte Hilb.
Nachlass Hans Pfeiffer.
Archiv zur Geschichte der Schweizerischen Frauenbewegung, Worblaufen, Switzerland.
Bibliothek der Israelitischen Cultusgemeinde, Zürich.
Bibliothèque Juive de Genève.
Leo Baeck Institute Library, New York.
Les Archives d'État de Genève.
Schweizerisches Bundesarchiv, Sektion Benutzung, Bern (Swiss Federal Archives).
The New York Public Library, Dorot Jewish Division.

PERIODICALS

Der Beginen: Newspaper of the Jewish Refugees in Switzerland.
Dos Vort, 1944.
Israelitisches Wochenblatt. Für die Schweiz, journal Israelite Suisse, 1941–46.
Über die Grenzen, Von Flüchtlingen für Flüchtlinge, 1944–45.

BOOKS, CHAPTERS, ARTICLES

Abella, Irving and Troper, Harold, *None is Too Many: Canada and the Jews of Europe 1933–1948* (Toronto: Lester & Orpen Dennys, 1983).

Albers-Schönberg, Heinz, *Die Schweiz und die jüdischen Flüchtlinge 1933–1945: Eine Unabhängige Studie* (Stäfa: Th. Gut Verlag, 2000).

Barbey, Mary Anna (ed.), *39–45, Les femmes et la mob: Récrits recueillis par Lucie Allaman, Jo Pellet, Françoise Ray, Evelyne Vaucher* (Carouge-Genève: Editions Zoé, 1989).

Bardach, Ann Louise, 'Edgar's List', *Vanity Fair* (March 1997), pp.255–69.

Bauer, Yehuda, *American Jewry and the Holocaust: The American Jewish Joint Distribution Committee, 1939–1945* (Detroit, MI: Wayne State University Press, 1981).

Baumel, Judith Tydor, *Unfulfilled Promise: Rescue and Resettlement of Jewish Refugee Children in the United States, 1934–1945* (Juneau, Alaska: Denali Press, 1990).

Bonjour, Edgar, 'Swiss Neutrality During Two World Wars', in J. Murray Luck (ed.), *Modern Switzerland* (Palo Alto, CA: Society for the Promotion of Science and Scholarship, 1978), pp.419–38.

Bornstein, Heini, *Insel Schweiz: Hilfs- und Rettungsaktionen sozialistisch-zionistischer Jugendorganisationen 1939–1946* (Zürich: Chronos, 2000).

Bower, Tom, 'Blood Money', *Sunday Times News Review*, 9 March 1997, pp.1–2.

Brusto, Max, *Im Schweizer Rettungsboot: Dokumentation* (München: Starczewski-Verlag, 1967).

Buffat, Françoise and Cohen, Sylvie, *Suisses et juifs: Portraits et témoinages* (Lausanne: Favre, 1998).

Camartin, Iso, Francillon, Roger, Jakubec-Vodoz, Doris, Käser, Rudolf, Orelli, Giovanni and Stocker, Beatrice (eds), *The Four Literatures of Switzerland*, translated by Eileen Walliser-Schwarzbart (Switzerland: Pro Helvetia Documentation-Information-Press, 1996).

Cattani, Alfred, *Die Schweizerische Flüchtlingspolitik 1933–1945* (Bern: Pro Libertate, 1999).

Charnley, Joy and Pender, Malcolm (eds), *Images of Switzerland: Challenges from the Margins* (Bern: Peter Lang, 1998).

Charnley, Joy and Pender, Malcolm (eds), *Visions of Utopia in Switzerland* (New York: Peter Lang, 2000).

Chiquet, Simone, Gygi, Fabio and Rychner, Marianne, '"... denn es ist alles wahr": – Fragen einer Ausstellung', in *Dossier 11, '... denn es ist alles wahr': Erinnerung und Geschichte 1939–1999* (Bern: Schweizerisches Bundesarchiv, 1999).

Codevilla, Angelo, *Between the Alps and a Hard Place: Switzerland in World War II and the Rewriting of History* (Washington, DC: Regnery, 2000).

Cohen, Beth B., *Case Closed: Holocaust Survivors in Postwar America* (New Brunswick, NJ: Rutgers University Press, 2007).

Croquet, Jean-Claude, *Chemins de passage: Les passages clandestins entre la Haute-Savoie et la Suisse de 1940 à 1944* (Saint-Julien-en-Genevois: La Salévienne, 1996).

Dame, Frederick William, *History of Switzerland* (Lewiston, NY: Edwin Mellen Press, 2001).

Dietz, Edith, *Freiheit in Grenzen: Meine Internierungszeit in der Schweiz, 1942–1946* (Frankfurt: Dipa Verlag, 1993).

Dreyfus, Madeleine, *Manifest vom 21 Januar 1997: Geschichtsbilder und Antisemitismus in der Schweiz* (Zürich: WoZ, 1997).

Ehrenberg, Wolf Zeev, *Emigrationen: Lebensstationen eines Juden aus Deutschland* (Zürich: Chronos, 2000).

Elon, Amos, 'Switzerland's Lasting Demon', *New York Times Magazine*, 12 April 1998, pp.40–4.

Fédération Suisse des Communautés Israélites, *Schweizerischer Israelitischer Gemeindebund, 1904–1954: Festschrift zum 50 jährigen Bestehen* (Zürich: Gemeindebund, 1954).

Fischer, Monika, *'Retten Sie wenigstens mein Kind': Zeitzeugen des Zweiten Weltkrieges berichten* (Zürich: Schweizerisches Jugendschriftenwerk, 2000).

Fivaz-Silbermann, Ruth, *Le refoulement de réfugiés civils juifs à la frontière franco-genevoise durant la Seconde Guerre mondiale: Suivi du mémorial de ceux parmi eux qui ont été déportés ou fusillés* (Paris: Klarsfeld Foundation, 2000).

Fluckiger, Pierre and Bagnoud, Gérard, *Les Réfugiés civils et la frontière genevoise durant la Deuxième Guerre mondiale: Fichiers et archives* (Genève: Archives d'Etat, 2000).

Frei, Annette, *Die welt ist mein Haus: Das Leben der Anny Klawa-Morf* (Zürich: Limmat Verlag Genossenschaft, 1991).

Friedenson, Joseph. *Heroine of Rescue: The Incredible Story of Recha Sternbuch who saved Thousands from the Holocaust* (New York: Mesorah, 1984).

Garlinski, Józef, *The Swiss Corridor: Espionage Networks in Switzerland During World War II* (London: J.M. Dent, 1981).

Gershon, Karen (ed.), *We Came as Children: A Collective Autobiography* (New York: Harcourt, Brace & World, 1966).

Goehrke, Carsten and Zimmermann, Werner G. (eds), *Zuflucht*

Schweiz: Der Umgang mit Asylproblemen im 19 und 20 Jahrhundert (Zürich: Verlag Hans Rohr, 1994).

Gosteli, Marthe and Zürcher, Regula (eds), *Vergessene Geschichte: Illustrierte Chronik der Frauenbewegung 1914–1963 / Histoire oubliée: Chronique illustrée du mouvement féministe 1914–1963* (Bern: Stämpfli, 2000).

Gross, Raphael, Lezzi, Eva and Richterf, Marc R. (eds), *'Eine Welt, die ihre Wirklichkeit verloren hatte ...': Jüdische Überlebende des Holocaust in der Schweiz* (Zürich: Limmat Verlag, 1999).

Guggenheim, Willy (ed.), *Juden in der Schweiz: Glaube, Geschichte, Gegenwart im Auftrag des Schweizerischen Israelitischen Gemeindebundes* (Küsnacht, Zürich: Kürz, 1982).

Gutman, Israel and Zuroff, Efraim (eds), *Rescue Attempts During the Holocaust: Proceedings of the Second Yad Vashem International Historical Conference, Jerusalem, April 8–11, 1977* (Jerusalem: Yad Vashem, 1977).

Gysling, Erich, König, Mario and Ganz, Michael T., *1945: Die Schweiz im Friedensjahr* (Zürich: Silva-Verlag, 1995).

Halbrook, Stephen P., *The Swiss and the Nazis: How the Alpine Republic Survived in the Shadow of the Third Reich* (Philadelphia, PA: Casemate, 2006).

Halbrook, Stephen P., *Target Switzerland: Swiss Armed Neutrality in World War II* (Rockville Centre, NY: Sarpedon, 1998).

Häsler, Alfred A., *Die geschichte der Karola Siegel: Ein Bericht* (Bern: Benteli, 1976).

Häsler, Alfred A., *The Lifeboat Is Full: Switzerland and the Refugees, 1933–1945*, translated by Charles Lam Markmann (New York: Funk & Wagnalls, 1969).

Häsler, Alfred A., *Wahrheit verjährt nicht: Eine Orientierung in schwieriger Zeit* (Frauenfeld: Huber, 1997).

Haymann, Emmanuel, *Le camp du bout du mond: 1942, des enfants juifs de France à la frontière suisse* (Lausanne: P.-M. Favre, 1984).

Herzka, Heinz Stefan, von Schumacher, A. and Tyrangiel, S., *Die Kinder der Verfolgten: Die Nachkommen der Naziopfer und Flüchtlingskinder heute* (Göttingen: Verlag für Medizinische Psychologie, 1989).

Hildebrandt, Irma, *In der Fremde zu Hause? Begegnungen mit Emigranten und Flüchtlingen in der Schweiz* (Basel: Verlag Herder Freiburg, 1982).

Hirsch, Peter, *Il disait s'appeler Peter Surava* (Genève: Edition Metropolis, 1998).

Hoerschelmann, Claudia, *Exilland Schweiz: Lebensbedingungen und*

Schicksale österreichischer Flüchtlinge 1938 bis 1945 (Innsbruck: Studien-Verlag, 1997).

Imhof, Kurt, Ettinger, Parik and Boller, Boris, *Flüchtlinge als Thema der öffentlichen politischen Kommunikation in der Schweiz 1938–1947: Beiheft zum Bericht die Schweiz und die Flüchtlinge zur Zeit des Nationalsozialismus* (Bern: Unabhängige Expertenkommission Schweiz, Zweiter Weltkrieg, 1999).

Independent Commission of Experts Switzerland – Second World War, Jean-François Bergier, Chairman, *Switzerland and Refugees in the Nazi Era* (Bern, 1999).

Kadosh, Sara, 'Jewish Refugee Children in Switzerland 1939–1950', in Elisabeth Maxwell and John K. Roth (eds), *Remembering for the Future: The Holocaust in an Age of Genocide* (London: Palgrave, 2001), Vol.2, pp.281–97.

Kägi-Fuchsmann, Regina, *Das gute Herz genügt nicht: Mein Leben und meine Arbeit* (Zürich: Verlag Exlibris, 1968).

Klarsfeld, Serge, *The Children of Izieu: A Human Tragedy* (New York: Harry Abrams, 1984).

Koller, Guido and Roschewski, Heinz, *Fluchtlingsakten 1930–1950: Thematisches Übersicht zu Bestanden in Schweizerischen Bundesarchiv* (Bern: Schweizerisches Bundesarchiv, 1999).

Kramer, Jane, 'Manna From Hell', *New Yorker*, 28 April and 5 May 1997, pp.74–89.

Kranzler, David, *My Brother's Blood: The Orthodox Jewish Response during the Holocaust* (Brooklyn, NY: Mesorah, 1987).

Kranzler, David, *The Man who Stopped the Trains to Auschwitz: George Mantello, El Salvador, and Switzerland's Finest Hour* (Syracuse, NY: Syracuse University Press, 2000).

Kreis, George, *Anti-Semitism in Switzerland: A Report on Historical and Current Manifestations with Recommendations for Counter-Measures*, edited by Doris Angst Yilmaz and translated by Lyn Shepard (Bern: Federal Commission Against Racism, 1998).

Kreis, Georg (ed.), *Switzerland and the Second World War* (London and Portland, OR: Frank Cass, 2000).

Kurz, Gertrud, *Unterwegs für den frieden: Erlebnisse und erfahrungen*, edited by Rosmarie Kurz (Basel: F. Reinhardt, 1977).

Laqueur, Walter and Breitman, Richard, *Breaking the Silence* (New York: Simon & Schuster, 1986).

Lasserre, André, *La politique vaudoise envers les réfugiés victimes du nazisme, 1933 à 1945* (Lausanne: Conseil d'État du canton de Vaud, 2000).

Lasserre, André, *Frontières et camps: Le refuge en Suisse de 1933 à 1945* (Lausanne: Payot, 1995).

L'Association des Archivistes Suisses, *Dossiers de réfugiés 1930–1950* (Bern: Les Archives Fédérales Suisses, 2001).

LeBor, Adam. *Hitler's Secret Bankers: The Myth of Swiss Neutrality during the Holocaust* (Secaucus, NJ: Carol, 1997).

Ludewig-Kedmi, Revital, Spiegel, M.V. and Tyrangiel, S. (eds), *Das Trauma des Holocaust zwischen Psychologie und Geschichte* (Zürich: Chronos, 2002).

Ludi, Regula, 'Waging War on Wartime Memory: Recent Swiss Debates on the Legacies of the Holocaust and the Nazi Era', *Jewish Social Studies* 10, 2 (2004), pp.116–52.

Ludwig, Carl, *Die Flüchtlingspolitik der Schweiz seit 1933 bis zur Gegenwart 1957* (Bern: Verlag Herbert Lang, 1966).

Makarova, Elena, *From Bauhaus to Terezin: Friedl Dicker-Brandeis and her Pupils* (Jerusalem: Yad Vashem, 1990).

Marrus, Michael, *The Unwanted: European Refugees in the Twentieth Century* (New York: Oxford University Press, 1985).

Moskovitz, Sarah, *Love Despite Hate: Child Survivors of the Holocaust and their Adult Lives* (New York: Schocken Books, 1983).

Mushg, Adolf, *Wenn Auschwitz in der Schweiz Lliegt: Fünf Reden eines Schweizers an seine und keine Nation* (Frankfurt am Main: Suhrkamp, 1989).

Newman, Ken, *Swiss Wartime Work Camps: A Collection of Eyewitness Testimonies, 1940–1945* (Zurich: NZZ Verlag, 1999).

Newman, Rafael, *Contemporary Jewish Writing in Switzerland: An Anthology* (Lincoln, NE: University of Nebraska Press, 2002).

Pavillon, Monique, *Les immobilisées: Les femmes suisses durant la Seconde Guerre mondiale: Essai historique* (Lausanne: Éditions d'en Bas, 1989).

Peiser, Gustave, *Une jeunesse de cristal: Souvenirs de ces temps-là, 1935–1945* (Genève: Georg, 2002).

Picard, Jacques, *Die Schweiz und die Juden 1933–1945: Schweizerischer Antisemitismus, jüdische Abwehr und international Migrations und Flüchtingspolitik* (Zürich: Chronos, 1994).

Picard, Jacques, *On the Ambivalence of Being Neutral: Switzerland and Swiss Jewry Facing the Rise and Fall of the Nazi State* (Washington, DC: United States Holocaust Memorial Museum Research Institute, 1998).

Regard, Fabienne. *La Suisse paradis de l'enfer? Mémoire de réfugiés juifs* (Yens sur Morges: Cabédita, 2002).

Renold, Andreas (ed.), *Kinderbilderwelter: Zeichnungen von Flüchtlingskindern 1945* (Zürich: Pendo Verlag, 2001).
Roschewski, Heinz (ed.), *Rothmund und die juden: Eine historische Fallstudie des Antisemitismus in der schweizerischen Flüchtlingspolitik 1933–1957* (Basel: Helbing & Lichterhahn, 1997).
Rotenberg, Alexander, *Emissaries: A Memoir of the Riviera, Haute-Savoie, Switzerland, and World War II* (Secaucus, NJ: Citadel Press, 1987).
Roth, John K., Maxwell, Elisabeth and Levy, Margot (eds), *Remembering for the Future: The Holocaust in the Age of Genocide* (New York: Palgrave, 2001).
Sarasin, Philipp, Wecker, Regina, Hug, Peter *et al.*, *Raubgold, Reduit, Flüchtlinge: Zur Geschichte der Schweiz im Zweiten Weltkrieg* (Zürich: Chronos, 1998).
Schmid, Max (ed.), *Schalom! Wir werden euch töten!: Texte und dokumente zum Antisemitismus in der Schweiz, 1930–1980* (Zürich: Eco-Verlag, 2000).
Schnauber, Cornelius, Sabalius, Romey and Stimpson, Gene (eds), *The Dream Never Becomes Reality: The United States in Contemporary Swiss Literature: An Anthology* (Lanham, MD: University Press of America, 1994).
Schom, Alan Morris, *The Unwanted Guests: Swiss Forced Labor Camps 1940–1944* (Los Angeles, CA: Simon Wiesenthal Center, 1998).
Schwarz, Urs, *The Eye of the Hurricane: Switzerland in World War II* (Boulder, CO: Westview Press, 1980).
Schweizerisches Bundesarchiv, *Die Schweiz und die Flüchtlinge/La Suisse et les réfugiés,1933–1945* (Bern: Paul Haupt, 1996).
Schweizerisches Bundesarchiv, *Zeitschrift des Schweizerischen Bundesarchivs: Studien und Quellen 22* (Bern: Verlag Paul Haupt, 1996).
Seliger, Kurt, *Basel–Badischer Bahnhof in der Schweizer Emigration, 1938–1945* (Wien: Österreichischer Bundesverlag, 1987).
Sibold, Noëmi, *'Mit den Emigranten auf Gedeih und Verderb verbunden': Die Flüchtlingshilfe der Israelitischen Gemeinde Basel in der Zeit des Nationalsozialismus* (Zürich: Pendo, 2002).
Siolino, Elaine, 'Sixty Years Later, Jews' Rescuer Seeks Swiss Pardon', *International Herald Tribune*, 15 January 2004.
Sperber, Manès, *Until My Eyes Are Closed With Shard*, translated by Harry Zohn (New York: Holmes & Meier, 1994).
Stadelmann, Jürg, *Umgang mit Fremden in bedrängter Zeit: Schweizerische Flüchtlingspolitik 1940–1945 und ihre Beurteilung bis heute* (Zürich: Orell Füssli, 1998).
Stauffer, Beatrice Uehli, *Mein Leben leben: Else Freistadt Herzka, 1899–*

1953: Zwischen Leidenschaft, Psychologie und Exil (Wien: Passagen Verlag, 1995).

Sutro, Nellie, *Jugend auf der Flucht, 1933–1948 Fünfzehn Jahre im Spiegel des Schweizer Hilfswerks für Emigrantenkinder* (Zürich: Europa Verlag, 1952).

Tartakower, Aryeh and Grossmann, Kurt R. *The Jewish Refugee* (New York: Institute of Jewish Affairs of the American Jewish Congress and World Jewish Congress, 1944).

Tugend, Tom, 'A Harsh New Blow for the Swiss', *Jerusalem Post*, 2 February 1998.

Vuilleumier, Marc, *Immigrants and Refugees in Switzerland: An Outline History* (Zurich: Pro Helvetia, 1987).

Wagner, Meir. *The Righteous of Switzerland: Heroes of the Holocaust*, edited by Andreas C. Fischer and Graham Buik (Hoboken, NJ: Ktav, 2000).

Waidson, H.M. (ed.), *Anthology of Modern Swiss Literature* (London: Wolff, 1984).

Waters, Donald Arthur, *Hitler's Secret Ally, Switzerland* (La Mesa, CA: Pertinent Publications, 1992).

Weber, Charlotte, *Gegen den Strom der Finsternis: Als Betreuerin in Schweizer Flüchtlingsheimen, 1942–1945* (Zürich: Chronos, 1994).

Weingarten-Guggenheim, Elisabeth, *Zwischen Fürsorge und Politik: Geschichte des Bundes Schweizerischer Jüdischer Frauenorganisationen* (Zürich: Limmat Verlag, 1999).

Westheimer, Ruth K., *All in a Lifetime* (New York: Warner Books, 1987).

Wiesel, Elie (ed.), *Die Zukunft der Vergangenheit: Beiträge zum Symposium des Schweizerischen Israelitischen Gemeindebundes vom 7 Oktober 1999 an der Universität Freiburg* (Zürich: Jüdische Rundschau Medien, 1999).

Wimmer, Adi (ed.), *Strangers at Home and Abroad: Recollections of Austrian Jews who Escaped Hitler*, translated by Ewald Osers (Jefferson, NC: McFarland & Company, 2000).

Wischnitzer, Mark, *Visas to Freedom: The History of HIAS* (Cleveland, OH: World Publishing, 1956).

Zeder, Eveline, *Ein Zuhause für jüdische Flüchtlingskinder: Lilly Volkart und ihr kinderheim in Ascona 1934–1947* (Zürich: Chronos, 1998).

Ziegler, Jean, *The Swiss, the Gold, and the Dead* (New York: Harcourt Brace, 1998).

INDEX

www.ingramcontent.com/pod-product-compliance
Lightning Source LLC
LaVergne TN
LVHW090901100726
842465LV00001BA/52
* 9 7 8 0 8 5 3 0 3 9 5 1 8 *